Southern
New England
for Free

Southern New England for Free

Steve Berman

Photography by
Adam Laipson

Leverett, Massachusetts

This book is dedicated to:

... all the people/teachers who've either consciously, unconsciously, or superconsciously guided my trip—

S.B.

... the Family of Humanity—

A.L.

Special Thanks To: Myron, Nevin, Jon, Dan, John, Jeff, Ronni, Bob, Candy, Susan, and Steve.

Introduction

I almost want to begin this introduction with a paean to New England; something like Pete Seeger's "This Land Was Made For You And Me" or even something a little *schmaltzier* like "America's" crescendoing end—"From sea to shining sea"—where visions of eagles and flapping-in-the-wind American flags are inevitably provoked. So—New England—from Cape Cod's sandy dunes to her divinely ignited fall foliage; from her misty little waterfalls tucked deep in the hills of western Connecticut to her tiny fishing villages along Rhode Island's rocky coast. New England (to move from this already too rhapsodic paean) is just a gas.

How to see New England? You can tour around, pay two-dollars-and-fifty cents admission charges, sleep in cramped motels, and eat quickie lunches at quickie diners. Or, you can tour around, pay *no* admission charges, and eat leisurely picnic lunches at leisurely parks.

Simply, this is a guidebook to *free* New England. Free and primarily *rural* New England. But the book is a lot more than just an extensive compilation of New England's "freebies," (though it's that, too). For entire days of free things to do have been carefully outlined here, and with the help of this book you can leave your house, spend a full day of free and interesting sightseeing, and then return home—hopefully more contented and enriched than frustrated and impoverished.

The book, then, is really about free.trips—free trips of one day's duration. And included here are historical trips, nature trips, architectural trips, art trips, and "chop suey" trips. (Chop suey trips are simply mad melanges.) And each trip includes unique locales, places often known only by a region's lifelong residents.

Not only are the trips thematically arranged (historical, art, nature, etc.), but each trip is also geographically circumscribed. So areas no larger than twenty square miles are covered by any of the one day excursions.

One word of caution, though, before you actually start free-tripping: Don't let the structure of each of the trips constrict you. Remember, this is *your* guidebook and use it however *you* like. All we've done is suggest possible sequences to see a group of free and related locales. But whether you choose to follow our trips exactly or whether you prefer to create some of your own variations, just keep in mind that all that matters—all that ever matters—is having a good time.

So drive carefully . . . and have a good trip.

Steve Berman

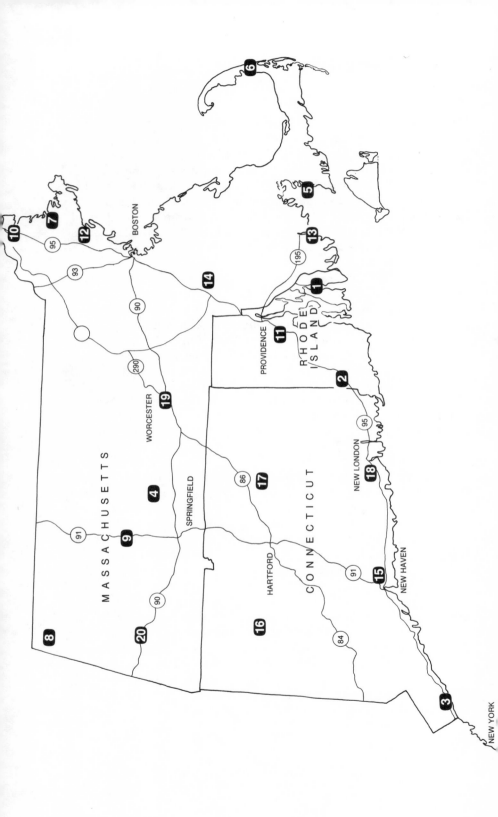

Contents

Nature Trips

1. Southeastern Rhode Island

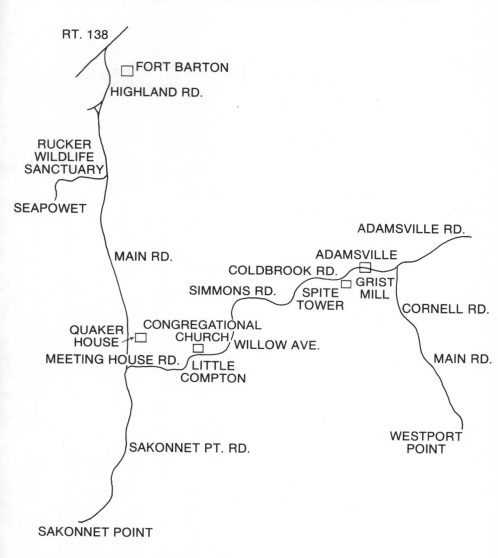

HOW TO GET THERE: From New York City take Route 95 towards New London, Conn. A little past New London, pick up Route 1, then Route 138 (which intersects with Route 77 not far from Tiverton, R.I.). From Boston take Route 24 South to Fall River, Mass. and then pick up Route 138 heading towards Tiverton.

9:00–10:30 A.M.	Fort Barton, Tiverton, R.I.
11:00– 1:00 P.M.	Rucker Wildlife Sanctuary, Tiverton, R.I.
1:00– 2:00 P.M.	Sakonnet Point, R.I.
2:00– 3:00 P.M.	Quaker House, Congregational Church and Cemetery, Little Compton, R.I.
3:00– 4:00 P.M.	Grist Mill and Spite Tower, Adamsville, R.I.
2:00– 5:00 P.M.	Westport Point, Westport, Mass.

An Off-Beat Nature Trip through Southeastern Rhode Island

If a psychiatrist were to ask you to free associate with the word "Rhode Island," the dialogue would probably go something like this:

PSYCHIATRIST: Rhode Island.
PATIENT: Newport!
PSYCHIATRIST: Rhode Island.
PATIENT: Providence!

But this smallest state in the Union, regardless of what our subconscious minds want us to believe, is a lot more than simply Newport or Providence. It's also scenic, remote fishing villages along the Sakonnet River and quaint, historic towns not yet widely publicized.

Fort Barton, located in Tiverton, Rhode Island, is this trip's first stop. The fort, built in the 1700's and strategically overlooking the Sakonnet River, served as an important look-out post during the Revolutionary War. British vessels threatening to attack Fall River, Massachusetts—a critical industrial center of the early American colonists—were kept a watchful eye on from the fort's observation tower. Today, that tower has been reconstructed and visitors to Fort Barton can see the entire length of the state from its heights.

The four acre park surrounding the fort includes a number of polished granite markings—each stone filled with interesting geographical and historical data. And an old cemetery, just beyond the fort's tower, is also on the grounds.

In addition, *Sin and Flesh Brook*, a tumbling stream that meanders through the eighty undeveloped acres abutting Fort Barton Park, is also worth visiting. Its gruesome name, derived from the even gruesomer historical moment when a Quaker was killed by a band of marauding Indians—his mutilated body then being thrown into the stream—belies the stream's present-day idyllic setting.

. . . Fort Barton, situated off of Route 138 on Highland Road (right

13

at the intersection of Highland Road and Lawton Avenue) is a unique combination of historical sites and lush natural settings.

Heading south from Fort Barton for a few miles on Route 77, you'll soon reach Sapowet Avenue. At Sapowet Avenue turn right and after driving a mile you'll spot the entrance to the *Rucker Wildlife Sanctuary*. The sanctuary's salt marshes, which attract all species of water fowl, make this Audubon-sponsored preserve a unique birding site.

The sanctuary has a number of trails that circle around the salt marshes, as well as paths that bring you to sandy and secluded coves.

(A wildlife sanctuary, unlike most tourist sites, is difficult to enjoy without a little knowledge of what you're seeing. So bring along a pair of binoculars and a good, easy-to-use field guide. . . . Roger Tory Peterson's *A Field Guide to the Birds—Eastern Land and Water Birds* has, for years, been the "birder's bible.". . . Without these tools, half the fun of a wildlife sanctuary—namely, the wildlife—will be missed. And one additional word of caution: Two people can go to a preserve and if there's only one pair of binoculars between them, someone's bound to get bored. So try to have a pair of field glasses for each member of your party.)

After lunching and birding at the Rucker Sanctuary, take a lei-surely ride along Route 77 South towards *Sakonnet Point*. (If you've brought along bicycles, this stretch of road starting at Little Compton, Rhode Island and ending at the tip of Sakonnet Point is a flat, tree-domed path which passes dozens of stately coastal mansions. The road is approximately five miles each way and makes for a perfect after-noon bike ride.)

Sakonnet Point, jutting out into Block Island Sound, is a small harbor filled with commercial and pleasure fishing crafts. Long, rock jetties stretching into the ocean and a nearby isolated beach make it a relaxing afternoon stop-over on this touring trip through southeastern Rhode Island. (If you're interested in observing just how Rhode Is-land's commercial fishermen go about their business, you can arrange with one of the boat's captains to board his ship and watch the fishing operations first-hand. Usually, you'll have to make these sort of reser-vations a few days in advance. But the experience of going out on one of these boats and watching New England's fishermen emptying their fish-filled nets is well worth the bother.)

Back in Little Compton, Rhode Island there are a number of

historical sites open to the public. *The Quaker Meeting House* on West Main Road (the local name for Route 77) was built in 1800. Its two front doors—one for men, the other for women—and its straight, rectangular shape—contrast sharply with Little Compton's other historical church—the slightly ornate *1704 Congregational Church*. The Congregational Church, with its high steeple and arched windows, is situated right in the center of the village of Little Compton.

Adamsville, another small town just a few miles northeast of Little Compton, has two fairly off-beat freebies. One is a *grist mill*, still in operation, whose milling stones were once powered by water power. Today, bizarrely enough, the mill is operated by an old, rusty Model-T engine. And not far from the grist mill is another of those classically and eccentrically New England oddities—a *spite tower* erected generations ago to separate the adjoining homes of two feuding Yankees. The tower, resembling a clock tower, has since been reincarnated as an artist's studio.

In the late afternoon, from April to November, you can watch lobster fishermen unloading their day's catch at the *Westport Point Wharf*. Westport Point, Massachusetts is only a few miles southeast of Adamsville, just over the Rhode Island-Massachusetts line. This small Massachusetts coastal village, with its fishermen anxious to recount their seafaring tales (like the fishermen who told me how he single-handedly harpooned two eleven-hundred pound swordfish in the same day) is a perfect place to both watch the setting sun and to end your day.

Some Tips on Budget Sightseeing

There are a number of ways to save money on a day of sightseeing. Other than using this book to guide you to free locales, carefully map out your journey to avoid toll roads. Costly turnpikes and dollar bridges can be relentless on your change purse. (And often, the alternative roads you'll be selecting—usually backroads that take you through a number of small towns—will be a lot more interesting than all those interminable and monotonous thruways.)

We've made it a point throughout this book to encourage picnic lunches. A family of four can buy a loaf of bread, some cheese, mustard, and tomatoes, and can easily eat for less than three dollars. . . . No tips, no tax, no waiting. . . . Just a simple meal enjoyed out-of-doors.

And one other money-saving tip: USE YOUR FEET. Don't always pile into the car when you only have to travel a quarter-of-a-mile to the next site. Save the gas and walk. Your car, your purse, and your body can all appreciate the exercise.

2. Central Rhode Island

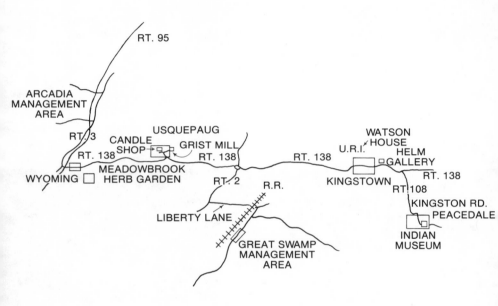

HOW TO GET THERE: From New York City take Route 95 to Wyoming, R.I. and then pick up Route 138 East. Route 138 goes right to the University of Rhode Island. From Boston, take Route 95 into Route 1.

10:00–11:00 A.M.	The Indian Museum, Peace Dale, R.I.
11:00–12:00 P.M.	The Watson House, The University of Rhode Island, Kingston, R.I.
12:00– 2:00 P.M.	Great Swamp Management Area, South Kingston, R.I.
2:00– 3:00 P.M.	Grist Mill, Candle Shop, Usquepaug, R.I.
3:00– 5:00 P.M.	Meadowbrook Herb Garden, Wyoming, R.I.
5:00– 7:00 P.M.	Arcadia Management Area, Escoheag, R.I.

A Nature Trip with Indians, Swamps, Herbs and Candles

I've always found museums to be "stuffy" environments; lifeless, frozen rooms struggling to preserve the past: and all of them with that feeling of "Do Not Touch" predominating. But *The Indian Museum* in Peace Dale, Rhode Island offers a refreshing exception to this usual pattern. It's a small and casual museum, with many of its displays openly exhibited—rather than entombed behind bulky, glass showcases.

In order to get into the museum, you'll have to first pick up the museum's key at the Peace Dale Public Library (Open Mondays through Fridays from 10–6:00 P.M., and Saturdays and Sundays from 10–5:00 P.M.)

Arrowheads, feathered bonnets, tomahawks, turtle rattles, drums, pottery, and even an Alaskan kayak are on display.

Heading out of Peace Dale on Route 108 North, it's only a two and a half mile ride to Kingston—the home of the *University of Rhode Island.*

On the University's campus, directly across from the library, is the *Watson House*—a simple farm-house typical of those built in Rhode Island in the late 1700's. Looms, spinning wheels, and colonial period furnishings are here on exhibit.... This eighteenth-century showcase is usually open to the public during the academic year. For special appointments (large groups, weekends) you can call 401–792–2730 or 401–792–2528.

The Helm House, also in the town of Kingston (right off of Route 138), is a home that was built in the early 1800's and today serves as an art gallery. Two weeks out of each month (closed January), the gallery is open—free of charge—to the public.

The Great Swamp Management Area is easily reached from

19

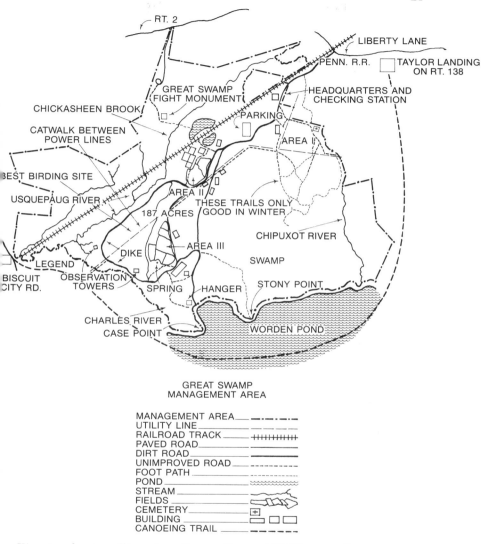

RT. 2

LIBERTY LANE

PENN. R.R.

TAYLOR LANDING
ON RT. 138

GREAT SWAMP
FIGHT MONUMENT

HEADQUARTERS AND
CHECKING STATION

CHICKASHEEN BROOK

PARKING

CATWALK BETWEEN
POWER LINES

AREA I

BEST BIRDING SITE

USQUEPAUG RIVER

AREA II

187 ACRES

THESE TRAILS ONLY
GOOD IN WINTER

CHIPUXOT RIVER

LEGEND

DIKE

AREA III

SWAMP

BISCUIT
CITY RD.

OBSERVATION
TOWERS

SPRING

HANGER

STONY POINT

CHARLES RIVER
CASE POINT

WORDEN POND

GREAT SWAMP
MANAGEMENT AREA

MANAGEMENT AREA	—..—..—
UTILITY LINE	— — — —
RAILROAD TRACK	++++++++++
PAVED ROAD	▬▬▬
DIRT ROAD	▬▬▬
UNIMPROVED ROAD	---------
FOOT PATH	·········
POND	〰〰〰
STREAM	
FIELDS	
CEMETERY	⊞
BUILDING	▭ ▭ ▭
CANOEING TRAIL	— — — —

Kingston by travelling six miles on Route 138 West until Route 138 intersects with Route 2. At this intersection turn left and drive one mile until you see a sign for the park area. Turning left at the sign (Liberty Lane), continue for two miles until you pass the first set of railroad tracks. Then, directly after these tracks, make a sharp right and the park's entrance is right down this road.

The Great Swamp Management Area is one of those nature spots that somehow manages to go unnoticed by travellers. Its 3,000 acres (most of them swampy) afford a genuinely singular experience to anyone willing to do just a little bit of hiking. The area's water impoundment, surrounded by an elaborate dike system, attracts a variety of water birds. (Green herons, ospreys, Canadian geese, quail, ducks, and dozens of other species.) There's a small catwalk, too, going across the impoundment that's safe to walk on, and it makes an excellent site to see some of these water birds close-up.

If you prefer fishing, bass and pickerel are always being caught right in the impoundment. And a canoe trip down the Chipuxet River, across the northern end of Worden Pond, then up the Charles River, is a full day's trip in itself. (See the diagram of the Great Swamp Management Area on the previous page.)

Nature trails, blueberry bushes, an old house foundation (said to be the home of Benedict Arnold's grandparents), and a sunken locomotive—all make the Great Swamp Management Area an off-beat and varied frip.* (Since hunters dominate the area from September 22nd through the last day of February, I'd recommend not visiting until the early spring or summer.)

Usquepaugh, a tiny, rural village approximately five miles from The Great Swamp Area (directly off of Route 138) has two interesting freebies: *Kenyon's Corn Meal Company*, a thriving grist mill which offers daily tours, and—just down the street from Kenyon's—the *Wood and Waxworks Craftsmen's Showroom*—where visitors can watch candle and furniture makers plying their crafts.

Your next stop on this nature trip through Rhode Island, (right off of Route 138 in the small town of Wyoming), is the *Meadowbrook Herb Garden*. And when you visit the herb garden, you're more than simply a sightseer. You're also a smellsmeller. . . . Let me explain.

As you approach the herb farm's 12 acres, your nose will instantly be filled with the scents of over 150 varieties of herbs. Sweet-smelling thyme, spicy basil, and stimulating mint will all quickly conspire to give you an olfactory rush the smells of which I can guarantee you've never experienced. The place is literally for the nose what the Louvre is for the eyes and what Tanglewood is for the ears . . . the ultimate smell trip!

Some would even argue it's the ultimate visual trip, as well . . . tall, delicate dill and fennel plants, with umbels of tiny yellow flowers; rare Korean mint bushes flowering late into the fall; and two-foot high rosemary plants, topped with clusters of pale blue flowers. So if you're

* *Frip:* free trip.

not instantly "blinded" by the smells at the herb farm, then certainly enjoy the sights as well. But for me it was almost exclusively my nose—not my eyes—that had a field day.

The farm consists of a gift shop, a cluster of greenhouses, a drying and storage shed (for harvested herbs), and acres and acres of well-cared-for herb plants. The farm is in full operation from mid-May to early October. (Open daily from 10–12:00 P.M., and from 1–5:00 P.M. Sundays—1–4:00 P.M.)

From the herb garden, head for *The Arcadia Management Area.* (Take Route 138 until it intersects with Route 3 North. Then turn right onto Route 3 and simply follow the signs to the park.)

This is an 11,000 acre complex which is part of the Appalachian Trail network. Fishing, swimming, nature trails, and a number of old cemeteries are in abundance throughout the park.

If you've been following our itinerary exactly, the Arcadia Management Area should be your last stop. And since you've been hiking and driving all day, I'd suggest using this final stop as a place to recoup your energies. Steppingstone Falls, at the northwestern corner of the park, with its large, rock slabs—surrounded by pools of calm water—is an ideal spot for this sort of pre-drive-home reflection.

HOW TO REACH STEPPINGSTONE FALLS

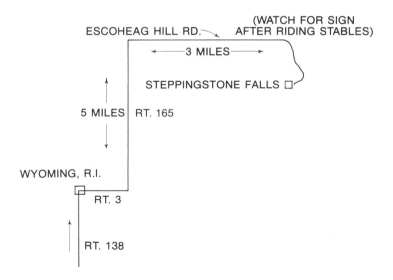

3. Southern Connecticut

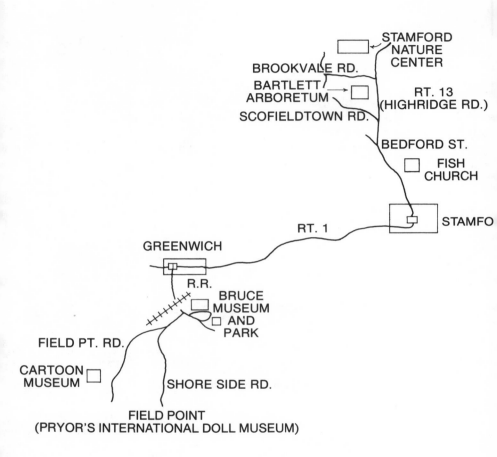

STAMFORD NATURE CENTER

BROOKVALE RD.

BARTLETT ARBORETUM

RT. 13 (HIGHRIDGE RD.)

SCOFIELDTOWN RD.

BEDFORD ST.

FISH CHURCH

RT. 1

STAMFO

GREENWICH

R.R.

BRUCE MUSEUM AND PARK

FIELD PT. RD.

CARTOON MUSEUM

SHORE SIDE RD.

FIELD POINT
(PRYOR'S INTERNATIONAL DOLL MUSEUM)

HOW TO GET THERE: From New York City take Route 95 right to the Stamford, Conn. Exit. From Boston take Route 90 into Route 86 heading towards Hartford. From Hartford take Route 91 into Route 95.

9:00–10:00 A.M.	First Presbyterian Church, Stamford, Conn.
10:00–11:30 A.M.	Bartlett Arboretum, Stamford, Conn.
12:00– 2:00 P.M.	The Stamford Museum and Nature Center, Stamford Conn.
2:00– 3:00 P.M.	The Bruce Museum, Greenwich, Conn.
3:00– 5:00 P.M.	The Cartoon Museum, The International Doll Library, Greenwich, Conn.
5:00– 6:00 P.M.	The Greenwich Archeological Foundation's Museum, Greenwich, Conn.

Greenhouses, Doll Houses, and God Houses

Southern Connecticut is a kind of de-militarized zone between New England's small rural towns and New York's ever-expanding megapolis. The entire area—stretching from Greenwich to Stamford, Connecticut is still amazingly New England in flavor, despite New York's encroaching frenetic vibes. So fortunately there are still spots in southern Connecticut where Gotham's mangled emanations can be totally avoided. And it's these undisturbed areas that this trip explores.

The First Presbyterian Church in Stamford, Connecticut (located at 1101 Bedford Street) is deceptive. From the outside, it resembles a drab concrete edifice—interesting only in that it was constructed to resemble a fish. But once inside, you're quickly transported to a serene, light-filled (and undeniably non-terrestrial) realm. The 23,000 pieces of one-inch-thick colored glass which cover the walls of the church, bathe the inner sanctuary in 86 subtle shades of light. The effect is the desired effect of most churches: to be spiritually uplifting.

Free tours of The First Presbyterian Church are offered every day except Sundays.

The Bartlett Arboretum, supervised by the University of Connecticut's College of Agriculture and Natural Resources, occupies 62 acres of countryside on the west side of State Highway Route 137 in North Stamford, Connecticut. Oak, maple, and hickory trees, along with a few scattered ash, birch, beech, and yellow poplar, grow abundantly in the arboretum.

Besides nature trails, a dwarf conifer garden, a bog walk, and hundreds of varieties of trees and flowering shrubs, there's also an in-resident indoor plant doctor always at the arboretum. You can bring your ailing asparagus ferns and philodendrons to the Bartlett Arboretum's plant doctor and free-of-charge he'll both diagnose your plant's disease and offer a remedy. (The spring and fall, of course, are the best times to visit the arboretum.)

To avoid paying a parking fee at the nearby *Stamford Museum and Nature Center* just walk along the path that leads to the Center from the arboretum. The museum and nature center, with its idyllic settings, will make a perfect spot for a picnic lunch.

The Stamford Museum, housed in a stately old English-Tudor manse, is primarily a natural history museum. But inside the museum there's also a contemporary art gallery whose eclectic shows are continually changing. And the nearby Stamford Nature Center is a perfect spot for kids. A non-claustrophobic zoo, where the animals are given enough room to freely roam, along with some nature trails and a swan-filled pond, makes this a choice spot for parents with-six-kids-in-search-of-an-activity.

Greenwich, Connecticut, just a few miles south of Stamford, has a number of free and off-beat museums. Least off-beat perhaps is the *Bruce Museum* in Bruce Park. (Open Monday through Friday from 10–5:00 P.M. Sundays 2–5:00 P.M. Closed Saturdays.) The museum is simply the Platonic Ideal of a "Natural History Museum." With its dark corridors and 3-D glass showcases (depicting such scenes as "The Pronghorn Antelope in Wyoming" and the "American Moose in Northern Maine"), the Bruce Museum manages to be a bit more dramatic than the Stamford Museum.

The Cartoon Museum (384 Field Point Road), just a few minutes drive from the Bruce Museum, is certainly one of the most specialized and more bizarre museums in all New England. The museum's mammouth Victorian manse houses the largest collection of original cartoon art in the world. Everything from the "Yellow Kid"—the first original comic strip ever to appear in print—to a complete portfolio of "Prince Valiant" drawings are on exhibition.

(If a museum dedicated exclusively to cartoon art strikes you as being a bit frivolous, just remember that besides jazz, cartoon art is the only other art form that both originated and flourished in America . . . and the least we can do for our native American art forms is house their histories in elegant museums.)

By calling 203–325–3808 and arranging a visit, you can view one

of the most extensive doll collections in the world. Samuel Pryor, a former executive vice president at Pan Am, is Greenwich's doll collector, and if you're genuinely serious about dolls, *Pryor's International Doll Library* is a must. Ancient Egyptian dolls and a vast collection of automatons (dolls with moving parts, figamajigs, and whachamacallits) are here on display. (Other than dolls, Pryor's acquisitive instincts also encompass early American penny banks, oriental furniture, porcelain, as well as first day covers.)

One last museum: *The Greenwich Archeological Foundation's Pre-Columbian Art Museum.* (By appointment only: 203–637–0215.) Here is a unique study collection of Mayan and Aztec pieces that both the specialist as well as the uninitiated can enjoy. Pottery fragments, jewelry artifacts, and stone carvings are all exhibited.

God houses, greenhouses, and doll houses should all make for a good solid day of fripping in southern Connecticut.

4. Central Massachusetts

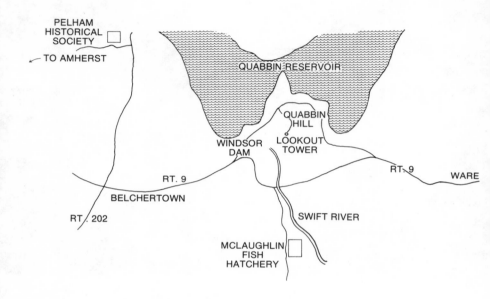

HOW TO GET THERE: From New York City take Route 95 into Route 91. Take the "Northampton-Route 9" exit off of Route 91 and then simply follow Route 9 to the Quabbin Reservoir-Windsor Dam entrance in Belchertown, Mass. From Boston, take Route 2 to Route 202. Route 202 intersects with Route 9 in Belchertown, Mass.

9:00–11:00 A.M.	The McClaughlin Fish Hatchery, Belchertown, Mass.
11:00–12:00 P.M.	Quabbin Park Cemetery, Ware, Mass.
12:00– 1:00 P.M.	Summit Tower and Picnic Area, Quabbin Reservoir, Belchertown, Mass.
1:00– 3:30 P.M.	Quabbin Reservoir Hiking Trails and Boating Facilities, Belchertown and Hardwick, Mass.
3:00– 4:30 P.M.	(Sat. only) Pelham Historical Society Museum, Pelham, Mass.

Quabbin Reservoir ... the Drowning of Four New England Towns followed by the Formation of Paradise

"The big shots over in Boston," the old-timer confided to me, "consider anything west of Worcester Indian country. So they think they can exploit the hell out of us." The elderly gentleman who was ranting and raving about all of Boston's no-nothing bureaucrats, then abruptly stopped in mid-conversation. "See all that water over there," he quickly said, pointing to a series of man-made lakes. "Well I once lived there until all them Boston fellows decided they needed some drinking water. And know what they did? They flooded out our towns and made themselves a reservoir; and all of us had to move."

Enfield, Dana, Greenwich, and Prescott, Massachusetts were the four small towns that were flooded out of existence back in the 1930's by Boston's Metropolitan District Commission. By building two massive earth dams and razing these four small towns, Boston's corps of engineers had successfully developed one of the world's largest reservoirs. But in the process they had also created resentments that were to linger for decades.

Today, *Quabbin Reservoir*—a 128 square mile reservation—despite the lingering bad vibes of a few displaced old-timers, is a paradisical freebie. And though the trip we've here laid out isn't strictly limited to the Quabbin Reservoir area, it's safe to say you could spend not only hours but *days* wandering around this sprawling reservation.

The "Windsor Dam Entrance" to Quabbin is right off of Route 9 in Belchertown. And just a little ways from this entrance (also off of Route 9) is the *McClaughlin Fish Hatchery*. The hatchery offers free tours everyday of the week but you'll have to call a few days in advance for reservations. (Their telephone number is: 413–327–7671.)

At the hatchery you can watch the entire maturation process of a

29

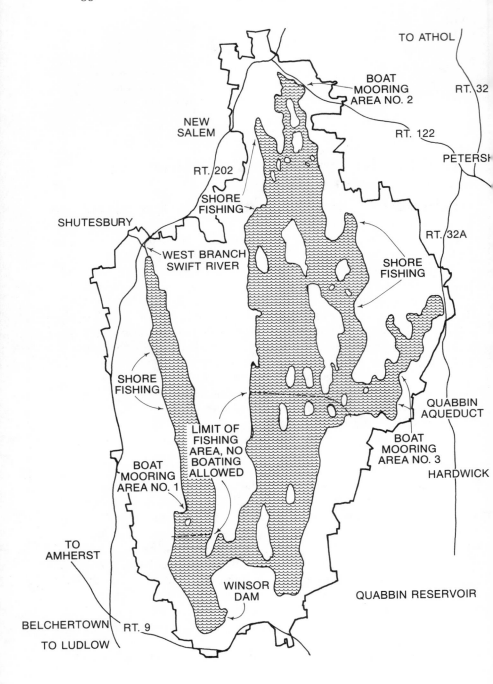

trout—from its infant egg-stage right up to the day when it's fully-grown and ready to be stocked into one of Massachusetts' reservoirs or lakes. Long, rectangular concrete pools, filled with thousands of darting speckled trout, gives the fish hatchery an aquarium-like atmosphere, making it an excellent place to bring kids.

When the thousands of WPA workers were building the reservoir back in the 1930's, there was one problem the engineers found particularly upsetting: how to dispose of all the cemeteries that were to be inundated. Finally, their slightly necrophilic solution was to dig up each of the 7,500 coffins and relocate them. *Quabbin Park Cemetery* resulted. . . . Today, if you don't find cemeteries too poignant a reminder of our human mortality, then certainly explore this burial ground. Lots of old, pre-Civil War gravestones can be seen here, and many of them have classically wry and grim Puritan epitaphs.

Near the "Windsor Dam Entrance" to the reservoir, the Metropolitan District Commission has its headquarters. You can pick up trail guides to the reservation here, along with some interesting historical and geographical pamphlets. (There are six nature trails located in the southern section of the park, and each one is well-marked on the trail guides.)

Quabbin Tower (or Summit Tower), atop Quabbin Hill, overlooks the entire Swift Valley. And at the base of the tower are about a dozen or so picnic tables. While cooking is prohibited in the area, picnic baskets are welcomed.

The places listed in this guidebook are all freebies. All along, we wanted to limit the book to off-beat, interesting, and *free* locales. But after some cursory soul-searching, we decided to tell you about one attraction that costs a dollar.

One George Washington, In-God-We-Trust dollar bill can get you a small boat (equipped with an outboard motor and three gallons of gas) that can cruise you around the more than 25 square miles of Quabbin Reservoir. There are three boat mooring sites—one in Belchertown, one in New Salem, and one in Hardwick, Massachusetts. (Generally, on weekends, early bird fishermen get to the boats first. But on just about any weekday afternoon, you shouldn't have too much trouble securing a boat. There's one catch, though, to this outrageously cheap, quasi-freebie: in order to rent a boat, you have to have a Massachusetts fishing license—which costs $8.50 a year. So either borrow one, or if you plan to visit Quabbin regularly, buy one! The boat will give you access to Quabbin's more than thirty deserted islands—and a boatride in the fall, when New England's foliage is divinely ignited, is well worth all the bother. . . . The boats are available from April to October.)

At the intersection of Route 202 and Amherst Road in Pelham, Massachusetts (a ten minute drive from the "Windsor Dam Entrance" of Quabbin Reservoir) is the *Pelham Historical Society's Museum*. This museum, open from 1:30–4:30 P.M. on weekends, is where the old replica of the *famed* Poison Oyster Stone can be found. (*Famed* is one of the museum's curator's words, not mine. Like 999,999 out of every 1,000,000 people, I too, had no idea what this *famed* stone was.) The stone's epitaph, though, indicts the wife of Warren Gibbs for murder, claiming she sprinkled some arsenic in her husband's oyster stew. And since most tombstone epitaphs are usually just a bunch of prosaic, laudatory drivel, this accusatory epitaph is, if not famous, at least, off-beat.

Quabbin Reservoir's more than 130 square miles can't be explored in just one day. A hit-and-run trip can give you little more than a "feel" for the place. So in order to really "see" Quabbin, you'll have to make at least three trips. . . . But however you schedule your visits, make sure to include at least one trip in the fall. For in late September and early October, Quabbin is one of the *thousand* (*seven* would just sound too hyperbolic) man-made wonders of our planet.

(The Quabbin Reservoir region, too, is perhaps the best American eagle habitat on the entire east coast.)

5. Western Cape Cod

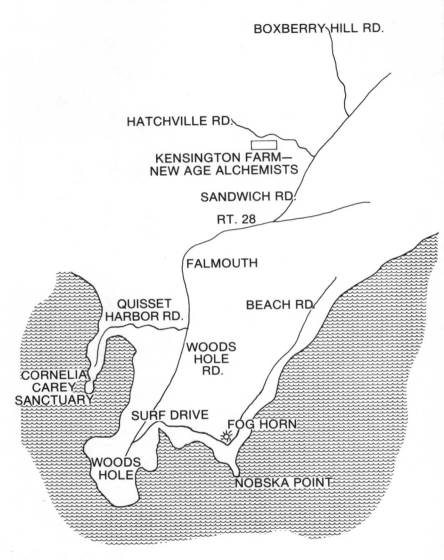

BOXBERRY HILL RD.

HATCHVILLE RD.

KENSINGTON FARM—
NEW AGE ALCHEMISTS

SANDWICH RD.

RT. 28

FALMOUTH

QUISSET
HARBOR RD.

BEACH RD.

WOODS
HOLE
RD.

CORNELIA
CAREY
SANCTUARY

SURF DRIVE

FOG HORN

WOODS
HOLE

NOBSKA POINT

HOW TO GET THERE: From New York City take Route 95 to Route 195 then get on Route 25. At the beginning of the Cape pick up Route 28 South into Hatchville, Mass. From Boston, take Route 3 into Route 28.

10:00– 2:00 P.M.	Kensington Farm (New Age Alchemists), Hatchville, Mass.
2:30– 3:30 P.M.	Cornelia Carey Sanctuary, Quisset, Mass.
3:30– 5:00 P.M.	Woods Hole Aquarium, Woods Hole, Mass.

Aquariums and Alchemists

Our world, many believe, is in trouble. Ecologically, the scientists are telling us, we're running a straight course towards self-destruction. Our energy reserves are greedily being exhausted, while both our food and water supplies are being dangerously polluted and depleted. . . . Certainly, not a very good condition for God's creation to be in.

Kensington Farm, in Hatchville, Massachusetts is attempting to do something about this "global suicide." (To reach the farm, follow the signs along Boxberry Hill Road to the Falmouth Playhouse. After the Playhouse, drive one-and-one-half miles to Hatchville Road and there make a left turn. The farm is then on your left-hand-side, about one-and-one-half miles up Hatchville Road.)

The New Age Alchemists (who work the farm) are a group of concerned scientists whose expressed aim is "to restore the land, protect the seas, and inform the earth sciences." To meet these ends, they've been experimenting with various alternative energy/farming/and living methods. Their farm is open to the public, and on Saturdays a free guided tour is offered.

The farm, with its windmills, organic gardens, and solar heaters, is really the pages of the *Whole Earth Catalogue* made manifest. (On weekdays, when the "alchemists" are busy working, they request that you explore their farm quietly and unobtrusively. But on Saturdays, you can bring your own lunch, work in the fields, and talk with each of the alchemists. . . . No doubt, a mellow and informative—and possibly prophetic—way to spend a Saturday morning.)

Leaving the farm and heading south on Route 28, (past the town of Falmouth), look for Quisset Harbor Road. At Quisset Harbor Road, turn right and stay on this road until you reach a small harbor filled with sailboats. Once near the harbor, park your car and follow the signs to the *Cornelia Carey Sanctuary*.

This sanctuary, overlooking Buzzards Bay, offers hours of mind-blowing seascapes. From a grass-covered promontory, you can see the Elizabeth Islands—a series of privately-owned islands whose inhabitants are among our country's wealthiest aristocrats. The sanctuary, as a stopover on your way towards the crowded and touristy town of Woods Hole, will be an appreciated cooling-out spot.

Woods Hole, Massachusetts, at the most southwesterly tip of Cape Cod, is the home of WHOI—the Woods Hole Oceanographic Institute—and the Marine Biological Laboratory. And in addition to it being an academic center, Woods Hole is also the main docking harbor for ferries heading to nearby Martha's Vineyard and Nantucket. As a result, droves of tourists and scholars intermingle along the narrow streets of this Cape town.

In Woods Hole, at the end of Water Street, there's the Aquarium—a free tourist site exhibiting nearly all the species of fish common to the area.... If crowds don't make you uncomfortable, then the Aquarium is a good spot to bring small children.

For those of you, though, who quickly find Woods Hole unpleasantly claustrophobic, take a drive along Surf Drive—a road which passes a number of public (yet surprisingly secluded) beaches.... Ending this trip on any one of these beaches is ideal.

On the Art of Visiting Cape Cod

Cape Cod can easily be declared a national disaster area on just about any hot, sunny summer weekend. Nearly half-a-million beach worshippers pour onto the Cape in July and August; and the effect is nothing less than lethally suffocating. All the roads, restaurants, gift shops, as well as the beaches are packed with people—with everyone trying to have a good time but with everyone incapable of moving. So a grandiose drag—complete with overheated cars, sunburned kids, and belligerent crowds—is all that's in store for you if you're not careful about when and how you visit the Cape.

... So if you can avoid it, *stay away from the Cape in the hottest parts of the summer.* The best time to visit is in the early Fall, after Labor Day—when all those romantic visions of long, wind-swept beaches and pounding surf are just that ... romantic visions. Otherwise the place is just an overpopulated, infernal nightmare; never right for beach-goers or romantics.

(But if you do find yourself on the Cape in the middle of a scorching weekend, just climb the highest dune, build a sandbag embankment, and there patiently wait for the fall before re-emerging.)

Trips 5 and 6 are a little off-beat. Each one is perfect for the early fall. (If for some contorted reason, though, you do give in to your masochistic urges and find yourself on the Cape on one of those hot, bumper-to-bumper summer days, then both trips can save your day from being a total disaster.)

... So enjoy the Cape—but enjoy it in the fall.

6. Eastern Cape Cod

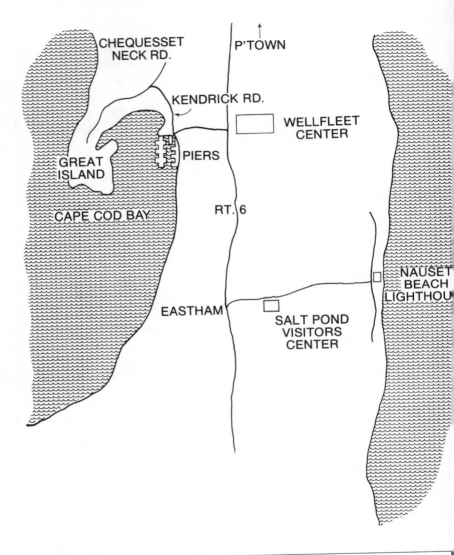

HOW TO GET THERE: From New York City take Route 95 past New London, Conn., and then pick up Route 1. From Route 1 get onto Route 138, which will lead into Route 177. From Route 177 take Route 6—which goes right to the Salt Pond Visitors Center in Eastham, Mass. From Boston, take Route 3 into Route 6.

Salt Ponds, Marshes and Islands

"Schlock," (one of those ultra-descriptive Yiddish words that's infil-trated into our everyday vocabularies), aptly characterizes five-eighths of Cape Cod. Half of the Cape is *pure* schlock—typified by the hun-dreds of bric-a-brac gift shops which crowd the main thoroughfares. Decade-old postcards, homemade marmalade, and felt hats festooned with rainbow-colored, squiggly embroidery are here *de rigueur*.

As for the more subtle gradations of "schlock," another eighth of the Cape consists of *hip* schlock—a species of schlock most perfectly embodied in a seascape that's "just right for the family room."

But "schlock" aside, three-eighths of Cape Cod does manage to remain untouched by grubby, greedy, tourist-hungry hands. And it's these undisturbed areas that's the *stuff* of this "Beach Trip To The Cape."

The Salt Pond Visitors Center, off of Route 6 in Eastham, Massa-chusetts is a smorgasbord of freebies. The Center (open 8–8:00 P.M.) offers a ten-minute movie which artistically explains the varied ter-rains and wildlife of the Cape. And a nearby museum, by using elabo-rate audio/visual exhibits, makes palatable some of the more esoteric geological and ecological principles that were involved in the Cape's early formation.

Self-guided, as well as guided nature tours, are also offered at the Visitors Center. The walks, which explore both salt ponds and nearby beaches (Coast Guard Beach and Nauset Light Beach) are all worthwhile outings.

Throughout the summer, daytime and evening lecture programs are given free-of-charge at the Salt Pond Visitors Center. To obtain a list of these free scheduled programs, you can write to the: Superintendent, c/o National Parks Service, U.S. Department of the Interior, South Wellfleet, Massachusetts 02663.

From Eastham take Route 6 towards Wellfleet. At the first sign for "Wellfleet Center" turn left and then head towards the Town Pier. At the Town Pier turn right onto Kendrick Road, and then make a left onto Chequesset Neck Road. Chequesset Neck Road, if you follow it for a few miles, will eventually lead to the entrance of *Great Island.*

Great Island—really a peninsula which dangles into Cape Bay (near Wellfleet, Massachusetts)—has more than six miles of National Seashore trails. Some of the trails meander around a tidal inlet that's an exceptionally good birding site. (Bring field glasses and field guides!) In addition, a Park's Department ranger offers a lengthy and well-informed walking tour of Great Island, and I'd recommend trying to schedule your visit to coincide with the tour. (Scheduling information for this tour can also be obtained by writing to the: National Parks Service in South Wellfleet.)

Before visiting the Cape, you might benefit by glancing at *Capre Cod,* a work by Henry David Thoreau. It was back in 1849 that Throeau made a walking tour of the Cape; and even today his travelogue offers some useful advice to the imaginative Cape traveller. Thoreau writes:

> In October, when the weather is not intolerably cold, and the landscape wears its autumnal tints, such as, methinks, only a Cape Cod Landscape ever wears, especially if you have a storm during your stay—that I am convinced is the best time to visit this shore.
> ... A storm in the fall or winter is the time to visit it. ...
> A man may stand there and put all America behind him.

7. Massachusetts' Cape Ann

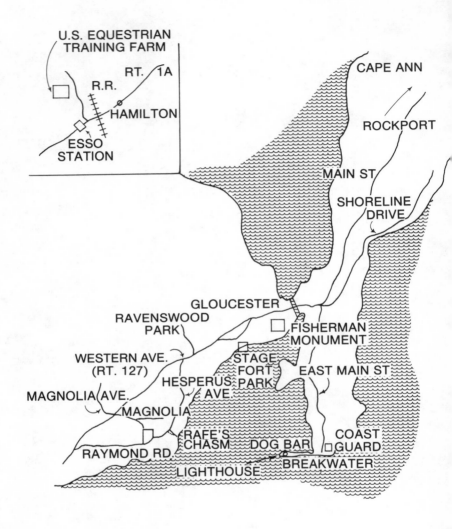

HOW TO GET THERE: From New York City take Route 95 into Route 91. Around Hartford, Conn. pick up Route 86, which will bring you to Route 90. Route 90 will intersect with Route 128. (Route 128 goes right into the North Shore area). From Boston, simply get on Route 128 heading towards the North Shore.

8:30–11:30 A.M.	The United States Equestrian Team, Hamilton, Mass.
11:30–12:30 P.M.	Rafe's Chasm, Magnolia, Mass.
12:30– 1:30 P.M.	Ravenswood Park, Magnolia, Mass.
1:30– 4:00 P.M.	Stage Fort Park, Fishermen's Monument, Fritz Hugh Lane House, North Shore Art Association, Dog Bar Breakwater, Eastern Point Lighthouse, Gloucester, Mass.
4:00– 5:00 P.M.	A Hit-and-Run Excursion to Rockport, Mass.

Coastal Tripping Along the North Shore

Massachusetts' "North Shore" region contrasts sharply with her schlock-infested southern coast: for the "North Shore" is strictly patrician turf, and plastic pop-culture hasn't yet become an epidemic.

Hamilton, Massachusetts, a blue-blood stronghold in the hinterlands of the North Shore—with its stylish manses and upper-crust hunt clubs—just wouldn't stand for any of McDonald's arches—even if they're golden. The town, to put it nineteen-fortishly, has "class."

Understandably, the *United States Equestrian Team* has its headquarters in Hamilton. (Equestrian is simply aristocratic for "horseman.") To reach the Equestrian Team's Training Farm take Route 1A through the town of Hamilton and once over the town's railroad tracks turn right at the Esso station. The farm is then just one mile up this road on your left-hand-side.

It's here where would-be U.S. Olympic team riders put their horses (and themselves) through rigorous daily paces. You can watch all the exercises and grooming procedures on just about any weekday (including Saturday) from 8–1:00 P.M. Sundays, though, the farm is closed to the public.

A tour of the grounds, which serves as an informative introduction to the aristocratic subculture of horsemanship, is also offered free-of-charge.

Your next stop, *Rafe's Chasm*, in Magnolia, Massachusetts (off of Hesperus Avenue) is a five-star freebie that owes five of its stars to its being hard-to-get-to. The chasm consists of mounds of granite boulders, all jaggedly piled along the shores of the Atlantic. As a secluded, coastal site it's ideal. But as a place to bring a family, because of the steep cliffs, forget it. (Its five-star rating, then, is only applicable to rock-climbing, mildly dare-devilish souls.)

Ravenswoods Park, also in Magnolia, Massachusetts (off of Western Avenue), is for the less adventurous. Here you can picnic in the park or hike along any of the nature trails that traverse the acres and acres of lush woods.

From Ravenswoods Park, the fishing port of Gloucester, Massachusetts is then only a five-minute drive along Route 127. And *Stage Fort*, directly off of Route 127 (also called Western Avenue) can be your first Gloucester freebie. The fort, the oldest defense built in the Massachusetts Bay Colony, has four Revolutionary War cannons—each strategically guarding the entrance to Gloucester Harbor.

Fortunately, because of its thriving commercial fishing industry, Gloucester manages to avoid being just another North Shore aristocratic showcase. So its artists and wealthy summer residents are more afterthoughts than social and economic fulcrums. And unlike Rockport—Gloucester's northern neighbor—swarming tourists just don't seem to swarm here quite so densely.

Fisherman's Monument, that by now classic statue of a weathered boatsman steering his ship (a statue that's been reproduced on nearly every seafood house's menu in America) is located at the western end of Gloucester's harbor. Assuming hackneyed, brass monuments are your thing, take a look.

Nearby, the *Fritz Hugh Lane House*, the home and studio of Gloucester's renowned nineteenth-century marine painter, is also open daily to the public. The house, built of massive granite blocks, is right in the center of Gloucester's commercial fishing wharves.

Gloucester is filled (fortunately not *inundated* like Rockport) with small art galleries. *The North Shore Art Association* (on East Main Street) is perhaps Gloucester's most extensive gallery. Its two floors exhibit works by regional as well as international painters.

(A FRIPPING HINT: *Every art gallery is a museum;* and as long as you're not overly desirous of any of the paintings or sculptures, you can enjoy hours of free tripping in any of these shops.)

Dog Bar Breakwater, and the nearby *Eastern Point Lighthouse*, both beyond Niles Beach (see map), can be reached only on weekdays. On summer weekends, a "Private—No Trespassing" sign prevents non-residents from reaching these sites. The breakwater—a long rock jetty—is an excellent coastal birding site. So be sure to bring field glasses and field guides.

The entire Cape Ann area (even Rockport—which was once a bona fide artist's colony but is today every tourist's favorite Kodak instamatic snapshot), is well worth exploring. By following Route 127A, which hugs the perimeter of Cape Ann, you'll pass many isolated inlets and coastal beaches.

Along Route 127A, do a little unstructured, unguided touring. (Halibut Point, Folly Cove, and Plum Cove are all good springboards for your free-form tripping.)

(The map of Cape Ann, which is distributed free-of-charge by the Chamber of Commerce in Gloucester, is an excellent guide to the entire North Shore region.)

8. Northwestern Massachusetts

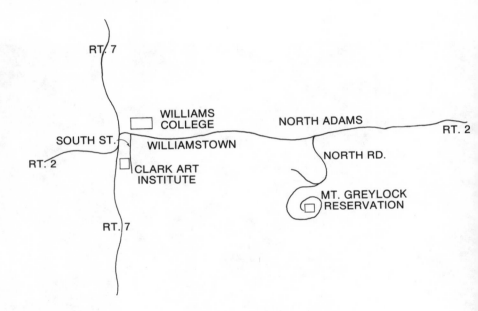

RT. 7

WILLIAMS
COLLEGE

NORTH ADAMS

RT. 2

SOUTH ST.

WILLIAMSTOWN

RT. 2

NORTH RD.

CLARK ART
INSTITUTE

MT. GREYLOCK
RESERVATION

RT. 7

HOW TO GET THERE: From New York City take the Taconic State
Parkway North to the Massachusetts Turnpike. From the turn-
pike pick up Route 7 North. Route 7 takes you right into the
North Adams/Williamstown area. From Boston, just take Route
2 West across the state of Massachusetts until you come into
Williamstown.

9:00–12:00 P.M.	Mount Greylock Reservation, North Adams, Mass.
12:00– 1:00 P.M.	Williams College, Williamstown, Mass.
1:00– 3:00 P.M.	Sterling and Francine Clark Art Institute, Williamstown, Mass.
3:00– 4:00 P.M.	Chapin Library, Williamstown, Mass.
4:00– 5:00 P.M.	Williams College Museum of Art, Williamstown, Mass.

Color Tripping in the Berkshires

(This is definitely a fall frip. You can, though, visit the Berkshires anytime of the year and it'll no doubt be equally enjoyable.)

Mount Greylock, Massachusetts' highest point (3,491 feet above sea level), in the town of North Adams (The Mount Greylock Reservation is situated right off of Route 2 West) is one of southern New England's genuine wilderness areas. Over 10,000 acres of forests comprise the reservation, and much of it is rugged mountain country. So hiking here is a lot more than just a stroll in the woods; it's genuine backpacking, including a few steep inclines and a number of rocky ledges.

There are trails leading from the base of the mountain right up to the paradisical top. And once on top, an observatory tower affords a panoramic vista of the entire Berkshire Range.

Only a few miles from North Adams is Williamstown, the home of Williams College and the Clark Art Institute. *Williams College*, a privately endowed, four-year liberal arts college presently has an enrollment of about 1,800 undergraduates. Its campus is a dignified blend of old ivy-covered buildings and modern stone structures; and just walking around the campus is an enjoyable way to spend a couple of hours. (At the school's Administration Building you can pick up a map of the campus.)

The Sterling and Francine Clark Art Institute (open Tues-Sunday from 1–5:00 P.M.) on South Street in Williamstown probably has New England's finest art collection. All the masters are here—Rembrandt, Rubens, Goya, Turner, Homer, Corot, Courbet, Daumier, Degas, and Renoir. Literally you could spend a week inside this vast marble building and still only manage to see half the works.

The museum is noted for its collection of Impressionists—works by Renoir, Monet, Degas, Sisley, Pissarro, Manet, and Toulouse-Lautrec. And indeed, the rich colors these Impressionists used in their works are almost as vivid as those you'll see on the trees on any sunny, fall afternoon.

On the Williams College campus there are also two worthwhile and open-to-the-public museums. *The Chapin Library* (on the second floor of Stetson Hall) is a rare book library with more than 17,000 volumes. There are first editions of many classic works of literature here—with authors ranging from Kipling to Melville. (The library is open daily, when the college is in session, from 9–12:00 P.M. and from 1–5:00 P.M. Closed Sundays.)

The Williams College Museum of Art (right off of Route 2) exhibits sculpture and painting from ancient Egypt and Assyria right up to the present. It's open daily from 10–12:00 P.M. and 2–4:00 P.M.; Sunday 2–5:00 P.M.

Historical Trips

9. Massachusetts' Pioneer Valley

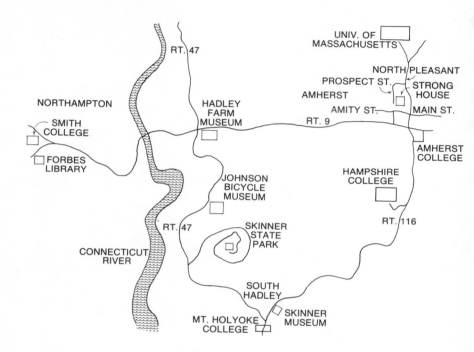

HOW TO GET THERE: This historical trip can easily be reached from New York City and vicinity by exiting at Interstate 91's "Northampton–Hadley" exit. From Boston, take the Massachusetts Turnpike to the Palmer exit and then follow signs for the University of Massachusetts.

10:00–11:00 A.M.	The Hadley Farm Museum, Hadley, Mass.
11:00–12:00 P.M.	Johnson's Bicycle Museum, Hadley, Mass.
12:00– 1:30 P.M.	Skinner State Park (Picnic Lunch) Hadley, Mass.
1:30– 3:00 P.M.	(Wed., Sun. only) Mount Holyoke College and The Skinner Museum, South Hadley, Mass.
2:00– 3:00 P.M.	The Strong House, Amherst, Mass.
3:00– 3:30 P.M.	The University of Massachusetts, Amherst, Mass.
3:30– 4:00 P.M.	The Mead Art Gallery and The Amherst College Campus, Amherst, Mass.
4:00– 5:00 P.M.	The Calvin Coolidge Memorial Room and Smith College, Northampton, Mass.

Smith College, Amherst and a Farm Museum

Most of New England's tourists, if they want to see early relics of America's history, will usually visit the restored colonial village at Sturbridge, Massachusetts. Along with Williamsburg, Virginia, it's "the place to go" to view 18th-century America. But if Sturbridge Village seems a little too expensive to your budget (or if it seems a bit too contrived for your taste), then our first historical trip should serve as an alternative to Sturbridge—an alternative that in addition to being totally free, will also, we feel, be fairly adventuresome.

The Hadley Farm Museum, located in Hadley, Massachusetts at the junction of Routes 9 and 47, is our first stop. Formerly an old 1782 hay barn, it is today filled to the rafters with thousands of early American farm and home-life implements. The museum's inventory is mind-blowingly extensive; making it one of New England's finest small museums. Ox carts, stage coaches, broom making machines, spinning wheels, cobbler's benches, wooden plows, and dozens of other colonial artifacts are all on display. . . . It's an informal museum with no padlocked glass showcases or uniformed security guards . . . an excellent introduction to colonial America.

The museum is open from May until October 12 from 10–4:30 P.M. Sundays 1:30–4:30 P.M. Closed on Mondays.

From there, following Route 47 for approximately four miles (towards South Hadley), you'll arrive at *Johnson's Bicycle Museum.* And like the Hadley Farm Museum, the bicycle collection is also housed in an old two-story barn. (As far as we know, no guidebooks—

not even the local *Hadley* tourist bulletin—lists this unique museum.)

The private collection includes bicycles dating as far back as the early 1800's. In fact, since the word "bicycle" only came into existence in 1869, you'll see in the barn dozens of two and three-wheeled "velocipedes"—the word that predated "bicycle."

(In addition to the bicycles—and even a *seven*-seat tandem bike is on display—you'll also see a rare 1901 Knox car parked in an adjacent garage.)

Assuming you're exactly following our itinerary, you should now be ready for some lunch. And if you've packed a picnic basket (which can be augmented by buying fresh vegetables at any of the small produce stands along Route 47), you can now head for *Skinner State Park*. (Open 10–8:00 P.M.). The park's entrance, right off of Route 47, is only a half-a-mile from the bicycle museum. (Incidentally, Hadley, Massachusetts, where the park is located, is world-famous for its tender asparagus. So if you're visiting in the spring or early summer, make sure to buy some freshly picked spears to take back home.)

Once in the park, take the park's steep and sinuous road as far as you can. For after a five-minute drive you'll be atop one of the highest

peaks in the entire Pioneer Valley. At this summit, you can explore the old boarded-up remnants of a turn-of-the-century hotel. Wealthy travellers back in the "gay-nineties" used to stop here for leisurely afternoons of dancing and boozing.

From the hotel's porch, the view is spectacular. Besides the Connecticut River meandering through the foothills of the Berkshires, you might even spot a bald eagle. A number of eagle sightings have already been recorded here. (And on one occasion, I even spotted two hang gliders slowly making their descent into a cow pasture.)

If you're travelling on either a Wednesday or a Sunday, *The Skinner Museum* in South Hadley, can be next on the day's agenda. The museum, located on Woodbridge Street, is open from 2–5:00 P.M. (Before visiting the museum, though, you might want to spend some leisurely time touring the *Mount Holyoke College* campus, which is situated in South Hadley. The school's ivy-covered stone buildings— both architecturally and historically unique—date as far back as the early 1700's.) Conveniently, the Skinner Museum and the college are only three miles from Skinner State Park.

The museum reflects the renaissance nature of Joseph Allen

Skinner—the gentleman who collected and donated many of the museum's pieces. Minerals, fossils, shells, medieval suits of armor, American Indian artifacts, pewter pieces, glassware, and two-hundred-year-old country furniture are all exhibited. Particularly interesting is an extensive collection of scrimshaw—or whale-bone carvings; a pastime indigenous to New England's nineteenth-century coastal towns.

Two carriage houses are also on the premises exhibiting sleighs, wagons, a stagecoach, and an eighteenth-century fire engine. . . . This museum is truly a rich melange of both American and foreign artifacts.

The Strong House, open 2–5:00 P.M., Tuesday through Saturday, is the second oldest home in Amherst, Massachusetts. From either South Hadley or the Skinner State Park, the home is no more than a fifteen minute drive.

Built in 1744, this colonial era manse is well worth a visit. Unlike most museums, whose artifacts are often too randomly squeezed into glass showcases, the exhibits here are all carefully displayed. Bedrooms, sitting rooms, and spinning rooms have all been undisturbed—so you can see them just as they were two-hundred-years ago.

Canopied beds, an 1823 rosewood piano, hand-painted wallpaper, patchwork quilts, and even a dress worn by the early American poet (and Amherst resident)—Emily Dickinson—are all on exhibition.

In the course of researching this guidebook it became apparent that sea captains abound in New England. It seems as if practically every small New England town has an old house where some retired sea captain spent his last years. And Amherst's Strong House is strictly in this tradition. As a result, ivory carvings from the East and bejewelled fans from France—all items brought back from world voyages—are also on display. . . . The Strong House, because it allows the imagination such an unadulterated glimpse into the past, is an ideal historical locale.

After this total immersion into eighteenth-century America, you might want to abruptly plunge yourself back into the twentieth century. So after visiting The Strong House, take a two-minute drive over to *The University of Massachusetts.* Huge monolithic, twenty-first century structures (which serve as classrooms and offices), along with a twenty-seven story library building, should easily "culturally shock" you back into the 1970's.

The Mead Art Building at Amherst College (open Monday through Friday from 10–12:00 P.M., then reopening from 1–4:00 P.M.), because it's air-conditioned and because it's historically rich, can be your next stop. Assyrian stone carvings, Flemish tapestries, Egyptian limestone sculptures, and ancient Greek pottery, are all on exhibit. In addition, the Rotherwas Room—formerly the 1611 banqueting hall of an English nobleman—has been perfectly reconstructed here. With its walnut panelling, sixteenth-century stained-glass windows, and elaborately ornamented oak mantelpiece, the room is perfect for a fantasy-filled, mid-afternoon rest. (Make sure, too, to at least view the *Amherst College* grounds. They're among the country's most impressive college campuses.)

. . . And what's an historical trip without at least one "George-Washington-slept-here" type inclusion. But since George Washington never did sleep here, you'll have to settle for Calvin Coolidge—a one-time mayor of Northampton, Massachusetts. Leaving Amherst on Route 9 and heading for Northampton, within fifteen minutes you'll arrive at *The Calvin Coolidge Memorial Room*, located in Northampton's Forbes Library.

Whereas taxidermists usually preserve great hunting moments by stuffing the quarry, historians do it by exhibiting (always behind a plush velvet rope) the chair and desk where a great man worked. So assuming you're sufficiently interested in where Calvin Coolidge sat or upon which particular oak desk he wrote, visit this collection of Coolidge memorabilia. Pictures, documents, election buttons, and gifts given to Coolidge during his presidency are all on display. Even a tape-recording of the thirtieth president's voice attempts to render ghost-like verisimilitude to the exhibit.

(Directly across the street from the Forbes Library, is *Smith College*—the country's oldest women's college. Here you can visit both the school's greenhouses and its art collection. The art gallery is open in July and August from 11–4:30 P.M., Tuesday through Saturday.)

. . . By now, you should either be historically sated or physically exhausted. So on the drive back home just sit back and enjoy the sunset—that, too, is free.

10. Northeastern Massachusetts

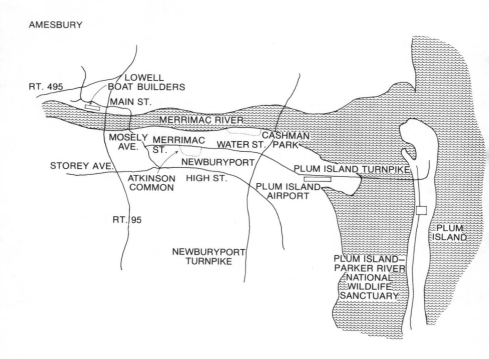

AMESBURY

RT. 495
LOWELL BOAT BUILDERS
MAIN ST.
MERRIMAC RIVER
MOSELY AVE.
MERRIMAC ST.
WATER ST.
CASHMAN PARK
STOREY AVE.
NEWBURYPORT
PLUM ISLAND TURNPIKE
ATKINSON COMMON
HIGH ST.
PLUM ISLAND AIRPORT
RT. 95
NEWBURYPORT TURNPIKE
PLUM ISLAND–PARKER RIVER NATIONAL WILDLIFE SANCTUARY
PLUM ISLAND

HOW TO GET THERE: From New York City use any one of the many routes to Boston. Out of Boston take Route 1A (a scenic coastal road) right to Newburyport.

9:00–12:00 P.M.	A Walking Tour of Newburyport, Mass.
12:00– 1:30 P.M.	The Plum Island Airport, Plum Island, Mass.
2:00– 4:00 P.M.	(or early morning in the summer) The Parker River National Wildlife Refuge, Plum Island, Mass.
4:00– 5:00 P.M.	Lowell Boatbuilders, Amesbury, Mass.

A Big Trek Through Massachusetts' Smallest City

Some towns live and die with their main industries. So once-prosperous New England manufacturing towns are today nothing but Industrial Age ghost-towns; their main streets only deserted shadows of a hey-day past. Other towns, despite the loss of their industry, somehow manage to maintain a dignified aura, almost as if their essence transcended the sum of their commercial enterprises. Or more simply, some towns have a "soul", others don't.

Newburyport, Massachusetts, (Massachusetts' smallest city), is one of those town's which managed to keep its soul despite the fact that it lost its main industry—shipbuilding—over a century ago. And today Newburyport is among New England's most soulfully historic areas.

A visit to the town should include a three-mile walk along High Street and its continuation, known as High Road, which runs into the adjacent town of Newbury. High Street is one of America's richest architectural treasures, with homes representative of practically every American period. The very early homes of the Seventeenth Century are of particular interest, and the outstanding examples of the Federalist period closely rival them. (Before you visit Newburyport write the: Tourist Committee, c/o Newburyport Chamber of Commerce, 21 Pleasant Street, Newburyport, Massachusetts—and ask for their well-planned walking tour of the city. Make sure to enclose a self-addressed stamped envelope.)

Besides the town's old churches, courthouse, and cemeteries, there are also two quiet picnic sites—*Moseley Woods*, at the crossroads of Spofford Street, Moseley Avenue, and Merrimac Street, and *Atkinson Common* at the north end of High Street. Both areas make relaxing sites for an afternoon lunch.

Old Newbury Crafters at 364 Merrimac Street, where silversmiths still ply their craft, and *Piel Craftsmen*, a store featuring ship models, also make unique side-trips for your tour of Newburyport.

Plum Island Airport on Plum Island Boulevard, is a small airport limited to privately-owned, propeller-driven planes. (The airport is only a five minute drive from the center of Newburyport.) Other than watching these lightweight planes taking off and landing, the airport also displays a number of antique WW II planes—including a German fighter plane and an English Tiger Moth. (And since most places displaying these sort of air history treasures usually charge a high admission fee, try to make it a point to at least briefly stop here on your way to the Plum Island-Parker River National Wildlife refuge.)

The *Plum Island-Parker River National Wildlife Refuge* (three miles east of Newburyport) consists of nearly 5,000 acres of unspoiled beach land. And since unspoiled, sans MacDonalds coastline is rapidly becoming an uncommon commodity, you'll have to get out to the refuge early in the morning if you expect to get in. Otherwise, because of the droves of sun-worshippers from Boston, you'll never get a parking space.

The refuge is positively *the best* birding site in the entire state of Massachusetts. Over *300* species of water and land birds have been spotted here, including thousands of migrating geese and ducks.

(At the entrance to the refuge—off of Sunset Drive—make sure to ask the parking attendant for the refuge's bird, fish, and mammal lists which were compiled by the National Parks Service.)

(And during the late summer and early fall, don't forget to pick wild plums and cranberries that grow along the beaches.)

As was suggested for the Cape Cod trips, visiting the refuge in the late fall or early winter can be a "multi-dimensional" experience. And day-tripping here in the winter—when there's snow on the ground and cross-country skiing is available—can easily be a peak experience. (For once you really open to the idea of visiting any of the locales listed in this book during their "off season," that whole concept of a place having an "off-season" will become ludicrous.)

The refuge offers swimming, fishing, hiking, skiing, plum picking, sunning, and birding. . . . So every season's an "on season" at Plum Island.

After leaving the refuge, head for Amesbury, Massachusetts, where the ancient and unfortunately disappearing art of shipbuilding is still being practiced on the shores of the Merrimac River. At the *Lowell's Shipbuilders* (right off of Amesbury's Main Street) you can watch small sturdy skiffs being assembled by hand. In our frantic "time-is-money/money-is-time" age, the experience is most refreshing.

11. Historical Rhode Island

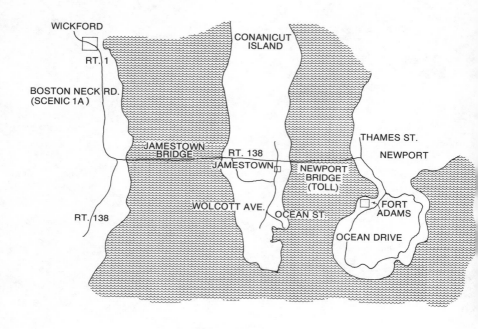

HOW TO GET THERE: Wickford, R.I., this trip's first stop, is easily reached from New York City by taking Route 95 East to West Warwick, R.I. From West Warwick take Route 1 South right into Wickford. From Boston, simply follow Route 95 South into Route 1.

9:00–11:00 A.M.	A Walking Tour of the Restored Colonial Village of Wickford, R.I.
11:30– 1:00 P.M.	World War I Bunkers, Fort Wetherill State Park, Jamestown, R.I.
1:30– 5:00 P.M.	Summer Estates, Touro Synagogue, Fort Adams, Vernon House, Mystery Tower, Artillery Company Museum, Newport, R.I.

From Colonial Austerity to Industrial Age Decadence

Wickford, Rhode Island, a small coastal village on the western shores of Narragansett Bay, has more well-preserved 18th century homes than any other village of its size in New England. Its streets are literally filled with dozens of steeply pitched gabled roof houses; all of them colonial era homes consisting of a massive central chimney surrounded by large, perfectly square rooms.

The village of Wickford, located in the town of North Kingston (directly off of Route 1A), is best seen by leisurely walking through its carefully laid out streets. It was back in 1709 that Lodowick Updike first planned the village (as a money-making, real estate development), and today, his original town plans remain virtually unchanged.

If you keep to the walking tour we've laid out, you'll get a nice feel for this old Rhode Island seaport.

Wickford's narrow, well-preserved streets (many of them still covered by brick) are a Pandora's Box for students of early American architecture. (The U.S. Department of the Interior's National Park Service publishes an inventory of all of Wickford's historic structures. As an in-depth guide, listing over forty homes, the pamphlet is invaluable. Copies of it can be seen at the Wickford Public Library.)

Probably most impressive of all of Wickford's historical sites is the *Old Narragansett Church* on Church Lane (see Walking Tour). It was originally built four miles southwest of Wickford in 1707 and was then moved to its present site in 1800. According to old records it was moved "between Tuesdays." The church is thoroughly austere, perfectly reflecting the somber personalities of the Puritans who built it. (Unlike the present-day garish edifices we construct to God, this church, besides having a surprisingly decorative door, lacks all external ornamentation.)

On Sunday mornings in August there's an open-to-the-public Vesper service at the church. During the service, the original, two-

65

A WALKING TOUR THROUGH WICKFORD, R.I.

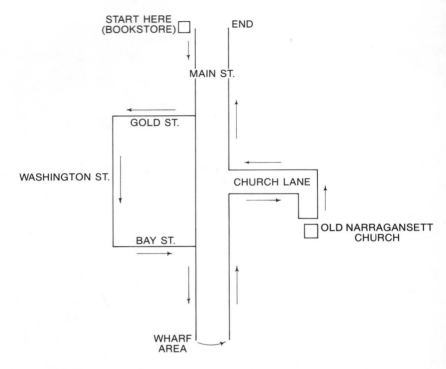

hundred-and-fifty-year-old silver chalice (given to the church by the Queen of England) is used.

Leaving Wickford on scenic Route 1A, head south and cross the Jamestown Bridge. Once over the bridge, you'll be on Conanicut Island. *Fort Wetherill State Park,* our second stop on this trip through Rhode Island, is then located at the southern most tip of the island. From the town of Jamestown, driving along Wolcott Avenue, it's approximately a two-and-a-half-mile ride to the park's entrance.

Fort Wetherill, open 6–11:00 P.M., overlooks the Rhode Island Sound—(as well as overlooking the summer home of Jackie O's family). The fort, which is right at the entrance to Narragansett Bay, served in both World Wars as a Navy redoubt. Two-foot-thick concrete bunkers and foot-wide gun mounts—all deserted—today can be seen. (Most of the abandoned fortifications are on the property of the Jamestown Highway Department and since they close their gates at 4:00 P.M., make sure to be out of the fort at least before 3:30 P.M.)

The park, with its small, isolated coves, all protected by grassy cliffs, also makes an ideal picnic and swimming site.

Newport, Rhode Island (right over the Newport Bridge from Jamestown) can become, if you're not careful, a tourist trap. The unavoidable Newport Bridge—with its phenomenal two-dollar toll—can be an inauspicious omen if you're not prepared to see this city for free.

To orient yourself to Newport, both historically and geographically, you might want to start your freebie tour of the city at the Chamber of Commerce (93 Thames Street). The Chamber of Commerce shows a free documentary movie, which, if you can transcend the commentator's too sugary voice, serves as a good, brief introduction to the town. Also at the Chamber of Commerce be sure to pick up an official visitor's map of Newport. This map, although exclusively listing places charging visitor's fees, is useful to the day fripper.

Not far from the Chamber of Commerce is the *Touro Synagogue*, the oldest Jewish house of worship in America. Designed by Peter Harrison, the most notable architect in mid-18th-century America, the synagogue is a perfect embodiment of Georgian-style architecture. The Touro Synagogue is open to the public from late June until Labor

Day from 10–5:00 P.M.—Monday through Friday; and from 10–6:00 P.M. on Sunday.

The Mystery Tower, between Mill Street and Pelham Street, as its name implies, is a mystery. Some claim it was built by the Vikings, others by the colonials. Whatever its origins, though, viewing it and trying to conjecture about its use is an interesting head-trip. (And head trips, naturally, are always free.)

From the tower, head northwest towards *Clarke Street;* for of all Newport's historic streets, it's Clarke that's the most densely populated with old, pre-Civil War structures.

At the corner of Clarke and Mary Street is the *Vernon House*, a 1758 building which served as General de Rochambeau's headquarters during the Revolutionary War. The building's facade, while constructed of wood, amazingly looks and *feels* like stone. ("Rustication," whereby wood is given a stone-like quality, is the term for this two-hundred-year-old building process.)

Next, continuing your walk down Clarke Street, just about in the middle of the block, is the *Artillery Company Museum*. The museum, housed in an 1836 stone armory, exhibits military uniforms from nearly every war we belligerent humans have ever engaged in.

(All of Newport's historic buildings—and there are over 420 pre-1830 structures throughout the city—are well-marked by identifying plaques. And if you really want to get into the histories of each of these sites, get out from any library a copy of Antoinette Downing's *Architectural Heritage of Newport*. This definitive text will make your walking tour through the city that much more informative and rewarding.)

Ocean Drive, a ten mile road that runs around the entire perimeter of the island, is, as they say in the vernacular, "a trip in itself." Not summer homes or summer cottages, but lavish mansions neatly crowd this winding path.

At the southwestern tip of the island, along Ocean Drive, at *Brenton Point State Park*, are the gutted-out remnants of an old, deserted estate. The estate's dilapidated stables, which overlook an abandoned, ocean-front polo field, are easily four times the size of any modern-day suburban spread.

Ocean Drive then aristocratically runs into one of America's wealthiest pockets—the gargantuan estates along Bellevue Avenue. Here is where those turn-of-the-century industrialists—the Morgans, Astors, and Vanderbilts—built their summer "cottages"—really monstrous Louis XIV showcases that never heard of the word "ostentatious." Most of these houses, many of them still occupied by families

whose surnames have become household words—Firestone, Eastman-
Kodak, Duke—snobbishly sit behind high concrete walls, and are
guarded by cadres of armed security guards. (By strolling along *Cliff
Walk*, which starts at Memorial Boulevard, however, you can glimpse
many of these repositories of wealth and power.)

After 4:00 P.M., head for *Fort Adams State Park.* (Before 4:00 P.M.,
you'll have to pay a parking fee!) The fort, among the largest seacoast
fortifications ever built in the U.S., has served as a military installation
for more than two centuries. Its history spans the years between the
Revolutionary War right up to World War II. There is a fee to tour the
inside of the fort but visitors can freely walk about the fort's outer
shell and grounds.

On the return trip home, to keep your mind off your aching feet,
just think of how you'll spend the twenty or thirty dollars you saved
today by avoiding paying any admission fees.

12. Massachusetts' North Shore

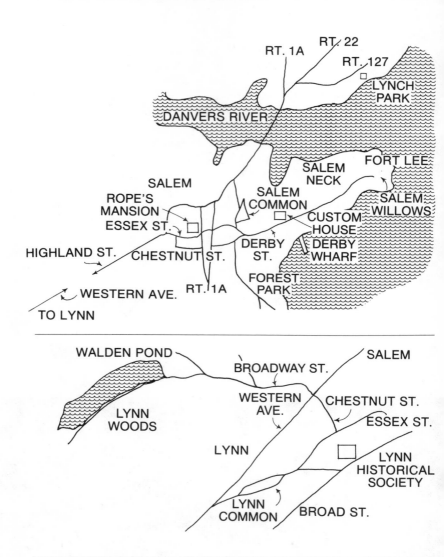

HOW TO GET THERE: From New York City take Route 95 into Route 91. Around Hartford, Conn. pick up Route 86, which will bring you to Route 90. Route 90 will intersect with Route 128. (Route 128 takes you right near Salem, Mass.). From Boston, simply get on Route 128 heading towards the North Shore.

10:00– 1:00 P.M.	Custom House, Derby Wharf, Ropes Mansion Garden, Salem Willows Carousel, Forest Park, Mansions Along Chestnut Street, Salem, Mass.
1:00– 3:30 P.M.	Lynn Historical Museum, Lynn Woods, Lynn, Mass.
3:30– 6:00 P.M.	Lynch Park, Beverly, Mass.

Where Witches and Angels Once Roamed

Salem, Massachusetts, where our sometimes intolerant Puritan fore-fathers executed nineteen witches back in 1692, is today trying to crassly cash-in on that gruesome event. 3-D museums reconstructing those infamous witch trials, along with hundreds of Halloween-type witches—their brooms whizzing across every billboard and store-front—threaten to make an historically rich town a bit too commer-cial. Nevertheless, Salem is worth a visit and fortunately, it still can be seen for free.

A sightseer who's determined not to spend any money in a town that caters to tourists has to exert a little discipline. The free tripper will inevitably be confronted with lines of tourists waiting to spend $3.00 at some museum: and it's those moments when discipline is necessary. Temptations to spend money in a town like Salem are simply omnipresent. But with a little restraint and some trust in this guidebook, your free trip, (nine-out-of-ten-times!), will prove more rewarding than any fifty-dollar-a-day extravaganza.

Admonitions aside, start your free tour of Salem at the *Custom's House* on Derby Street. A brief movie is shown here and it serves as a good introduction to the town's history.

The Custom's House, built in 1819, was where the novelist Nath-aniel Hawthorne worked as a shipping clerk. In fact, in his introduc-tion to his classic work "The Scarlet Letter," Hawthorne wrote at length about this very building.

Just behind the Custom's House are the old *warehouses* and *scale houses* where imported goods coming into Salem's port were stored and weighed.

And directly across the street from the Custom's House is *Derby Wharf*—where Revolutionary War "privateers" returned to Salem with shiploads of treasures (treasures which had been captured from commercial British fleets). A tour of both the Custom's House and the *Wharf* is given free-of-charge by park rangers.

While you'll have to pay to see the *Ropes Mansion* on Essex

Street, its formal gardens are open to the public. Salmon and red-colored canna—a flower that grows wild in Australia—and purple cone flowers make this garden a visual treat on just about any summer day.

Nearby, along *Chestnut Street*, huge eighteenth and nineteenth-century mansions can be seen. These houses, all privately owned, were formerly the manses of Salem's well-to-do merchants and shipmasters.

If you follow Derby Street in a southeasterly direction, you'll eventually reach *Salem Willows*. (Incidentally, the map of Salem which is freely distributed throughout the town is an extraordinarily clear and easy-to-use guide.) The Willows is a small amusement park—replete with teeth-rotting cotton candy and Kool-Aid snow cones. And while I don't usually recommend these sort of skooter car/rural Coney Islands to day trippers, Salem Willows does have one spectacle that makes it semi-worthwhile . . . a hand-carved, antique carousel—complete with red dragons spewing green flames and pink rhinos with monkeys on their backs. The carousel, decorated with

original paintings of all the U.S. presidents (from Washington to McKinley), is a nice resting spot before leaving Salem. (Also, at the other end of the city is *Forest Park*, where parking and swimming are both free.)

Local historical societies and town museums are usually run by pleasant golden-agers. Old-timers seem to congregate at these museums—congregating not as over-the-hill artifacts but rather as useful and animated raconteurs. The *Lynn Historical Museum* on 31 Broad Street in Lynn, Massachusetts (just a few miles south of Salem on Route 107) is such an admixture of historical exhibits and elderly storytellers . . . and a guided tour through the museum conducted by any one of these old-timers is a joyful (if somewhat eccentric) odyssey into Lynn's past. Ornate, turn-of-the-century hair combs, glass ship models, shoes manufactured in Lynn—which was one of the largest shoe-producing towns in New England—are all on display. (The Lynn Historical Museum is open 1–4:00 P.M. daily. Closed on Saturdays, Sundays, and holidays.)

Not far from the museum is *Lynn's Woods* (see map). Back in the 1800's, it was the largest municipal park in the U.S. Today, as a picnic site—especially for a picnic site on an historical trip through northeastern Massachusetts—it's unsurpassed. A large stone observation tower, resembling a medieval fortress, along with "Dungeon's Rock"—a cave said to be the hiding place for a priceless buried treasure—add some historical folklore to this lush site.

Whosoever enters here let him beware
For he shall nevermore escape nor be
free of my spell.

With these portentous words greeting you as you enter the formal gardens at Beverly, Massachusetts' *Lynch Park*, you'll soon be inside a calm, almost monastic setting. (Route 22 takes you right into the town of Beverly. But once in the town, because the roads leading to the park are vaguely marked, you'll have to ask someone for specific directions.) The gardens, overlooking the Atlantic Ocean, are filled with grape arbors and roses. A "presence," too, some say, also fills the area.

(If you sit in the center of the gardens for a few quiet moments before heading home, you just might find out whose *spell* it is that you'll "nevermore escape nor be free of. . . .")

A visit to the park on a fall Saturday or Sunday, will usually find a

dozen men of Italian descent playing *bocci ball*—Italy's ancient cross-pollination between billiards and bowling. The games are played at a high intensity so be prepared for some profane tongue-flapping and a lot of good-natured ribbing.

A Spiritual Trip into Sightseeing

Sightseeing involves two variables: sites and seeing. And since most of this book deals with "sites," I'd like to now just say a few words about "seeing."

Two people can go on any of the twenty trips included in this book, and at the end of a trip, one person might have had a good time, while the other a bad time. Yet they both saw the same "sites." So logically there couldn't have been anything about the sites themselves to account for the different reactions. The different reactions to the same trip, therefore, have to somehow stem from *how they saw* the identical sites . . . and not from *what they saw*. Which all sounds very obvious and *is* very obvious.

Only thing is, most of us don't want to admit it: most of us don't want to admit that having a good time is more a function of *how* we see something than of *what* we actually see. Why? Simply, I think, because it's a lot easier to blame something external for our bad times (like a site, a spouse, a teacher, anything!) than to blame ourselves.

Which is really a tragedy (maybe *the* tragedy) since it's usually a lot easier and a lot less painful to change ourselves (our "way of seeing") than to change all the external things we're always assuming to be the causes of our bad times. Or as some Zen masters like to say: You can pave all the streets in the world with rubber or you can just wear rubber sandals.

Now admitting this little essay on sightseeing has already taken its turn for the philosophical, I'll just add one more superficial/profound remark: That if *how* we see determines whether or not we have a good time, then learning "how to see" is maybe the most important thing we as people can do.

So *how* we see the sites this guidebook mentions is ultimately a lot more important than the sites themselves.

HINT: Any religion worth its scriptures should be in the business of teaching us "how to see"—how to see clearly without greed, lust, jealousy. . . . But that's another trip and now back to the guided trips.

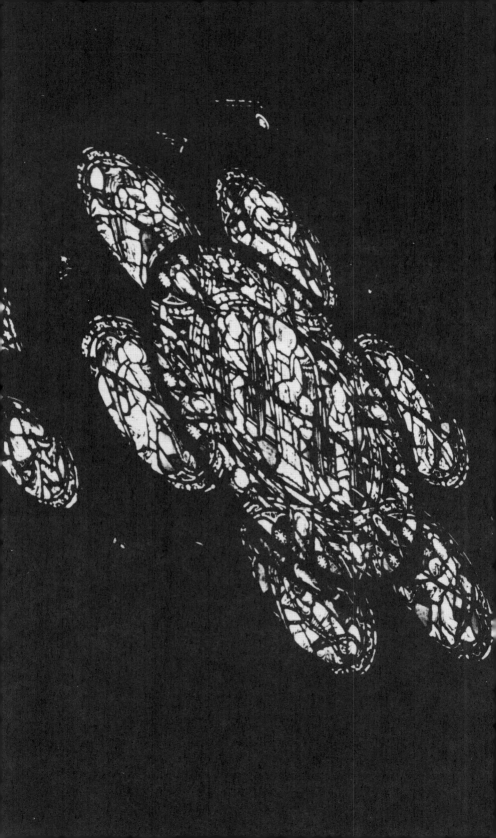

Architectural Trips

13. Southeastern Massachusetts

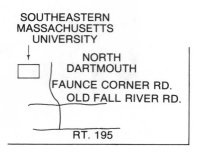

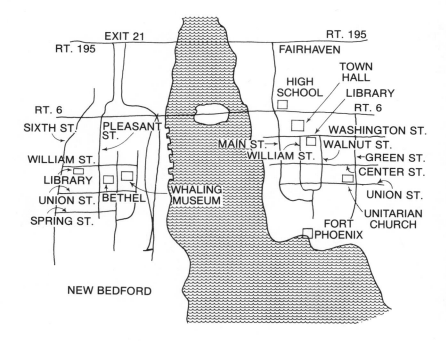

HOW TO GET THERE: This architectural trip is easily reached from New York City by travelling Route 95 to New London, Conn. and there picking up Route 1. Take Route 1 towards Jamestown, R.I., then pick up Route 138, followed by Route 177. Route 177 takes you right into North Dartmouth, Mass. . . . this trip's first stop. From Boston take Route 24 to Taunton, Mass. and there pick up Route 140.

9:00–10:00 A.M.	The Campus of Southeastern Massachusetts University, N. Dartmouth, Mass.
10:00–12:30 P.M.	A Walking Tour of a Whaling City, New Bedford, Mass.
12:30– 1:30 P.M.	Fort Phoenix, Fairhaven, Mass.
2:00– 6:00 P.M.	Fairhaven's Four Architectural Extravaganzas, Fairhaven, Mass.

Sixteenth-Century English Gothic to Tomorrow's Concrete

The campus of *Southeastern Massachusetts University* in North Dartmouth, Massachusetts was the brain-child of Paul Rudolph—one of America's most imaginative contemporary architects. Rudolph's powerful designs revel in concrete textures; everything from smooth, cylindrical shapes to coarse, brick-like patterns.

Massive overhangs, the thorough lack of any wood, and the nearly irresistible urge to touch his buildings, all contribute to the unusualness of Rudolph's structures. As both functional, useful designs, as well as art objects, these buildings are unsurpassed.

I'd suggest touring both the inside and outside of each of SMU's buildings. For from any angle, either externally or internally, Rudolph's designs are continually offering new perceptual blasts.... A paradoxically fluid, architectural vision all cast in solid concrete!

Next, to reach *New Bedford, Massachusetts* from SMU get on Route 195 East and take exit 21; then follow signs to the "Whaling Museum."

New Bedford, from the 1830's right up to the First World War, was a whaling port. Huge ships would start what was often a three-to-four-year whaling voyage from her harbor.

It was whale oil—the end product of boiling whale blubber—that these voyages sought. And in the mid-1800's, when most of our nation's lamps burned whale oil, a barrel of this fuel ran as high as $60.00. By the 1920's, though, just about the time kerosene was becoming popular, a whaler was lucky if he could unload his catch at $8.00/per barrel. (Ironically, New Bedford was one of the first American cities to build an *oil* refinery.)

A good place to start your free tour of this whaling city is the *New Bedford Public Library* on William Street. The library's *Melville Whaling Room* is an historical archive, containing logs and account books of some of New Bedford's great whaling voyages. If you study

79

these account books, you'll find that it took anywhere from $15,000 to $25,000 to outfit a whaling ship. Usually, a dozen or more investors would put up this initial money, and they'd be the ones to split two-thirds of the total catch. Crew members would then split (their "lays" or shares being determined by their respective skill and seniority) the remaining one-third.

From the library, head for the *Seamen's Bethel* on Johnny Cake Hill (near Water Street). The bethel, opened in 1832, is the finest example of this period's architectural design. Here, too, is where Herman Melville—the part-time whaler and immortal author of *Moby Dick*—attended Sunday morning church services.

Across the street from the Seamen's Bethel is the New Bedford *Whaling Museum*. And though this museum charges an admission fee, you can peak in through the doors to see the largest ship model in the world—a complete and accurate model of the "Black Lagoda," a whaling ship typical of those which sailed out of New Bedford in the 1850's.

A walk around New Bedford's *wharf area*, with its fleet of fishing boats and old stone edifices, is a leisurely way to end your stop-over in this whaling seaport. (To reach the wharf area turn left at the foot of Johnny Cake Hill). . . . (At the Visitor's Information Center on Water Street, you can pick up a copy of the "Moby Dick Trail"—a small pamphlet which includes a map along with a number of descriptive blurbs about some of the wharf-area buildings. The pamphlet makes for easy day tripping through New Bedford's streets.)

Fort Phoenix in Fairhaven, Massachusetts is this trip's suggested picnic site. (From New Bedford take Route 6 East over the Acushnet

River Bridge. Once over the bridge, turn right on Green Street and follow Green Street until it dead ends at the fort area.) The fort, with its iron cannons, was destroyed by British troops back in 1778 but was quickly rebuilt in less than two years. Today it offers an excellent view

of the Acushnet River (and unfortunately it also affords a naked look at New Bedford's less-than-beautiful industrial skyline). . . . Still, it manages to make a perfect spot for a mid-afternoon rest.

Henry Huttleston Rogers was rich . . . very rich. In fact, he was one of John D. Rockefeller's partners at Standard Oil. As a result, the town of Fairhaven, Massachusetts—where Henry grew up—is nothing less than Roger's architecturally-splendid mausoleum.

At the turn-of-the-century, Henry Rogers decided it was time to make his bid for immortality. So at his sole expense, he had four magnificent buildings constructed at his birthplace . . . a French Gothic town hall, an Italian Renaissance library, a sixteenth-century English Gothic church, and an Elizabethan-style high school. Each of these structures—lavish in both their design and execution—while not definitely insuring Rogers the immortality he sought, are nevertheless among the best and least known free sites in all New England.

You can start your tour of Fairhaven's buildings at the *High School* (on Main Street). This 100-foot-high limestone and granite structure is filled with hand carvings, exquisite murals, and French plate glass windows.

From the High School, the *Fairhaven Town Hall*, with its second

82

floor ballroom, can be your next stop. (At the Selectman's office in the Town Hall, get permission to tour the building.) The plush ballroom, with its "windows" or portal-shaped pieces of glass with hand-etched historical scenes, shouldn't be missed.

Fairhaven's Unitarian Memorial Church, a vast, vaulted-ceilinged Gothic church, is reminiscent of those to be seen in Europe. It is, to use the tired epithets of generations of traveller writers, a "breathtaking" and "magnificent" structure. Soft, pastel-colored Tiffany stained glass windows depicting the Nativity (along with self-aggrandizing windows portraying Henry Roger's children) abound. Intricate Bavarian wood carvings, Italian marble floors, and even an original leaf from Gutenberg's bible are also to be seen here. This church, on a one to ten scale, is a number ten Freebie. Tours of the church are given every day from 2–4:00 P.M., except on Sundays.

Last, the *Millicent Library* (across the street from the Town Hall)—an Italian Renaissance structure—houses a number of off-beat items. Letters of Mark Twain's (who was a friend of Henry Rogers), a Samurai sword from Japan, and a complete collection of Fairhaven historical memorabilia are all included.

. . . Fairhaven, Massachusetts . . . where architecture buffs can give Henry Rogers some of that immortality his ego so lavishly sought!

14. Easton, Massachusetts

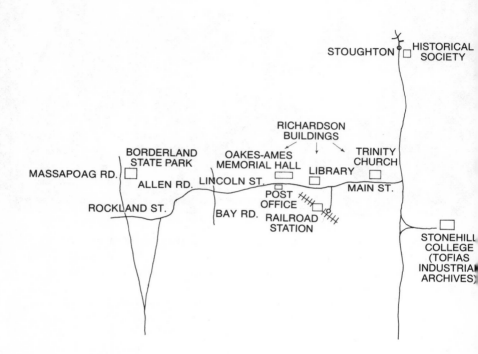

HOW TO GET THERE: From New York City take Route 95 all the way to Attleboro, Mass. Near Attleboro pick up Route 123 which takes you into Easton, Mass. From Boston, take Route 138 right into the center of Easton.

9:00–11:00 A.M.	The Buildings of Henry Hobson Richardson, North Easton, Mass.
11:00–12:00 P.M.	Unity Church, North Easton, Mass.
12:00– 2:00 P.M.	Borderland State Park, Easton, Mass.
2:00– 4:00 P.M.	Stonehill College, Easton, Mass.
2:00– 3:00 P.M.	(Wed. only) The Stoughton Historical Museum, Stoughton, Mass.

The Ames Family: Or How Big Business Shovels Its Profits into a Small Town

When Oliver Ames started to forge shovels back in the late 1700's, he probably sometimes fantasized—while working in his blacksmith's shop—that his business would mushroom into an international corporation. Probably on his frequent and thought-filled horse-and-wagon treks into Boston (where he sold his first, crudely-made shovels), Ames began to seriously realize the money-making potentials of his shovel business. And fueled by the realization, along with an unrestrained entrepreneurial spirit, Ames was soon energetically mass-producing his shovels. So by 1850, when more than sixty per cent of all the shovels used in the world were stamped with an Ames trademark, Oliver Ames had officially become the "shovel Baron."

Ames' descendants, born as it were with golden shovels in their mouths, became (as many of the super-rich become), art and charity enthusiasts. And combining these two avocations, they commissioned a series of buildings for their home town—buildings that were to be designed by the day's most renowned architect—Henry Hobson Richardson.

Richardson, a teacher of Louis Sullivan (who was the father of the modern skyscraper), worked primarily in stone. His buildings, with their cavernous arches over the doorways, are among the most powerful examples of nineteenth-century American architecture. (Richardson, incidentally, was the architect who designed Boston's famous Trinity Church.)

Five of Henry Richardson's buildings are in the town of North Easton: The *Oliver Ames Free Library*, located on Main Street; the *Oakes Ames Memorial Hall* (at Post Office Square); the *Gate Lodge*, on Elm Street; the *Gardener's Cottage*, also on Elm Street; and the *Old Colony Railroad Station*, on Mechanic Street. Each building offers a unique variation on Richardson's singular architectural style.

The Ames Library is decorated with bizarre gargoyles—all creations of Stanford White, the most famous nineteenth-century de-

signer of ornament. The Memorial Hall was landscaped by Frederick Olmsted, the same landscape architect who designed New York's Central Park. The Gate House, noted for its narrow, eyebrow windows, is the present-day home of one of Oliver Ames' fortunate descendants. And the Railroad Station, always a favorite among students of architecture, houses a museum exhibiting some of Easton's historical memorabilia.

The *Unity Church*, another of Oliver Ames' gifts to the town of North Easton, was built in 1875. It was designed by John Ames Mitchell, who was later to give up architecture to become an editor at *Life Magazine*.

The church's stained-glass windows were done by John LaFarge, the foremost stained glass artist in America in the late 1890's and early 1900's. And an elaborate oak screen, hand-carved by Johannes Kirchmeyer—a Hungarian artist—surrounds the pulpit. (To view the inside of the church, you'll have to make previous arrangements with Mrs. Luke—617–238–6663.)

After touring North Easton's architectural sites, head for *Border-land State Park*. (The park's main entrance is on Massapoag Avenue. From North Easton take Lincoln Street west across Bay Road, bearing right onto Allen Road. Then take a right from Allen onto Rockland Street, finally taking another right onto Massapoag. The park's free parking area is then a half-a-mile from this intersection.)

Formerly the estate of Oakes and Blanche Ames (more of Oliver's blessed descendants), Borderland is today a state park. The estate's ivy-covered stone mansion—open to the public on Sundays—is a totally fire-proof structure. Its floors are an unbelievable solid mass of concrete, over 14-inches thick.

The best time to visit Borderland is on an uncrowded weekday. For on just about any weekday afternoon, the estate's 1,250 acres are deserted. You can play tennis on the estate's courts, ride bikes throughout the park's paths, and fish in any of the ponds.

Stonehill College, whose administration building was the former home of Frederick L. Ames—still another of Oliver Ames' karmically blessed scions—houses the *Arnold B. Tofias Industrial Archives*. These archives contain the complete paper history of the Oliver Ames Shovel Company. Account books, payroll records, wage and production data, technical information, and sales records are all stacked in over 2,000 linear feet of shelf space. As an historical document reveal-

ing the inner workings of a pre-Civil War American business, the archives are invaluable. (Also on exhibit at Stonehill's Administration Building is an extensive collection of the different types of shovels manufactured by the Ames Shovel Company.)

If this day's dosage of the Ames family has you a bit sated, take a drive over to the *Stoughton Historical Society Museum*, in Stoughton, Massachusetts (Open Wednesday—2–4:00 P.M.; Thursday—7–9:00 P.M.; and Sundays—10–12:00 P.M.). From North Easton, Route 138 North takes you right into Stoughton. Like most small towns, Stoughton was never blessed with any multi-millionaire philanthropic industrialists. So its museum is just a simple, down-home collection of town memorabilia.

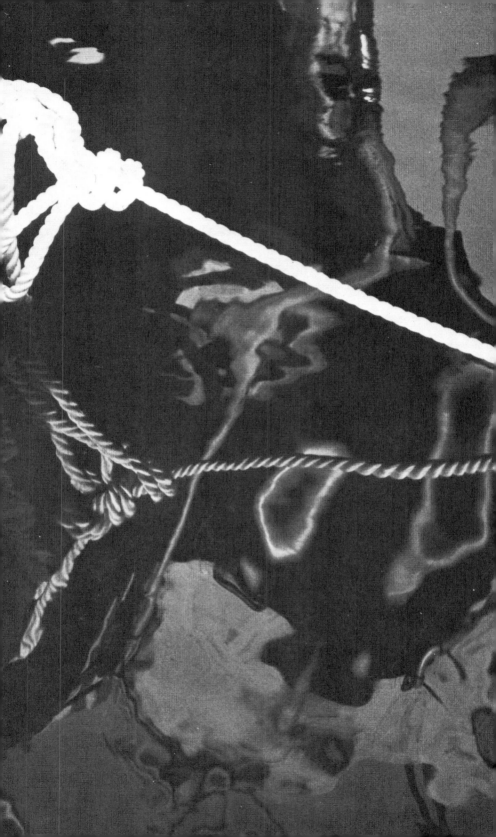

Art Trip

15. New Haven, Connecticut

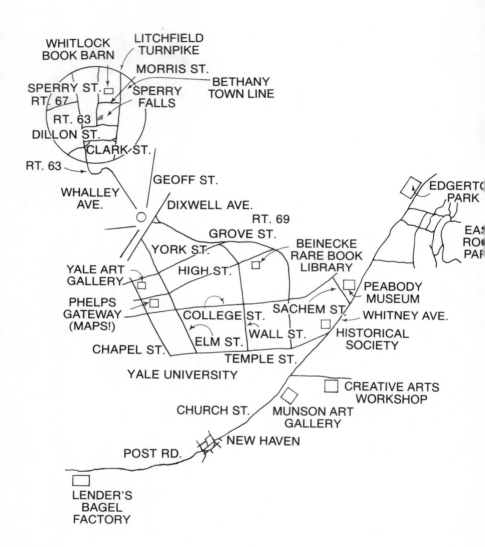

WHITLOCK BOOK BARN

LITCHFIELD TURNPIKE

MORRIS ST.

SPERRY ST.
RT. 67

SPERRY FALLS

BETHANY TOWN LINE

RT. 63

DILLON ST.

CLARK ST.

RT. 63

WHALLEY AVE.

GEOFF ST.

DIXWELL AVE.

RT. 69

GROVE ST.

YORK ST.

HIGH ST.

BEINECKE RARE BOOK LIBRARY

EDGERTON PARK

EAST ROCK PARK

YALE ART GALLERY

PHELPS GATEWAY (MAPS!)

COLLEGE ST.

SACHEM ST.

PEABODY MUSEUM

WHITNEY AVE.

WALL ST.

HISTORICAL SOCIETY

CHAPEL ST.

ELM ST.

TEMPLE ST.

YALE UNIVERSITY

CHURCH ST.

MUNSON ART GALLERY

CREATIVE ARTS WORKSHOP

POST RD.

NEW HAVEN

LENDER'S BAGEL FACTORY

HOW TO GET THERE: From New York City take Route 95 right into New Haven. From Boston take Route 95 all the way across Massachusetts and Rhode Island. Route 95 then takes you right into New Haven.

9:00–10:00 A.M.	Lender's Bagel Factory West Haven, Conn.
10:00–12:00 P.M.	A Walking Tour of Yale University, including The Art Gallery and The Beinecke Rare Book and Manuscript Library, New Haven, Conn.
12:00– 1:30 P.M.	Historical Society and The Peabody Museum, New Haven, Conn.
1:30– 2:30 P.M.	Edgerton Park and East Rock Park, New Haven, Conn.
2:30– 4:00 P.M.	Munson Gallery, Archetype Photography Gallery, Creative Arts Workshop, New Haven, Conn.
4:00– 6:00 P.M.	Whitlock Book Barn and Sperry Falls, Bethany, Conn.

Where Van Gogh
Busily Munches Bagels
Sitting Atop a Reconstructed Dinosaur

One warning before you even begin this trip: Don't expect to see New Haven in a day. Just trip leisurely and lightly.

Why include a bagel factory in a trip that's supposed to be reserved for art? Simple. Because bagels are art.

Now that statement isn't meant to be purposefully enigmatic; it's simply a statement of fact. And again, baking bagels *is* a genuine art . . . one requiring both skill and creativity.

If you've already accepted my bagel-as-art thesis without any intellectual reservations, then you'll also have to accept this following statement: that Murray Lender, the president of *Lender's Bagel Bakery*, is the Picasso of the bagel world. For Lender was nurtured on, influenced by, and always respectful of the bagel. Bagels are in the man's blood.

Over forty years ago, Murray's father started baking bagels in New Haven. Today, a half-a-century later, Murray heads his family's business and he's thoroughly enamored/obsessed with his product. For Murray, bagels aren't just "petrified donuts" or "Brooklyn jaw breakers" or as Buddy Hackett sometimes jokes "midgets' toilet seats." For Murray Lender, bagels are art.

You'll see bagels being produced at the rate of 1,500 dozen/per hour at Murray's factory. And if Murray happens to be your guide, you'll never again forget that bagels are the only product in the baking industry that have to be both baked and boiled. . . . Not a terribly

apocalyptic fact but Murray always manages to get palpitations over that bit of bagel trivia.

(You'll have to call or write ahead of time for a tour of the operations. Write: Lender's Bagel Bakery, Post Road, West Haven, Connecticut 06516.)

Yale University, New Haven's bastion of ivy-covered erudition, offers free guided tours of its campus. During the academic year, beginning on the first day of classes, one-hour tours leave from Phelps Archway on the Old Campus (on College Street opposite the Green) at 10:00 A.M. and 2:00 P.M., Monday through Friday; at 11:00 A.M. and 2:00 P.M. on Saturdays; and at 1:30 P.M. and 3:00 P.M. on Sunday.

During the summer, once Yale's commencement is over, general

94

tours are conducted every day at 9:15 A.M., 1:30 P.M. and 3:00 P.M., except Sundays, when the tours are at 1:30 P.M. and 3:00 P.M.

The tour is an excellent overview of this historically and architecturally rich campus. (A pamphlet entitled "A Walking Tour of Yale" which is available at Phelps Gate for $.10 also serves as a good guidebook for those of you who prefer to cruise around the campus on your own.)

The Yale University Art Gallery on 1111 Chapel Street is the oldest university art museum in the western hemisphere. Its eclectic collection includes works from nearly every national school of art, as well as pieces from virtually all the important periods in art history. The gallery is open Tuesday through Saturday from 10–5:00 P.M., Sundays 2–5:00 P.M. Closed Mondays.

The facade of the *Beinecke Rare Book and Manuscript Library* (on Wall Street), a building designed by Gordon Bunshaft (the architect who designed the United Nations building), consists of translucent one-and-one-fourth inch thick marble slabs. When sunlight pours into the building, first filtered through these slabs, the inner lighting effect is *meta-physical.* The library houses many rare and priceless manuscripts, and among them are the Gutenburg Bible and Audubon's complete folios.

New Haven's Historical Society (114 Whitney Avenue) is open Tuesday through Friday from 10–5:00 P.M. and from 2–5:00 P.M. on Saturday and Sundays. Colonial era furniture, silver and pewter pieces, antique dolls, and a variety of other historical relics are on display.

The Peabody Museum which charges no admission fee on Monday, Wednesday, and Friday, is Yale University's natural history museum. Besides the usual animals-in-their-habitat box displays, the Peabody also houses one of the world's most extensive and impressive collections of dinosaurs.

Having toured the bagel factory, Yale University, and the Historical Society and Peabody Museum, you can now head for either *Edgerton Park* or *East Rock Park* for a picnic lunch. Edgerton Park is a small park off of Whitney Avenue (entrance on Edgefield Road) and was a former estate. East Rock Park, a much larger area located at the eastern end of New Haven, has a number of nature trails along with extensive picnicking facilities.

Your afternoon in New Haven can be spent two ways: you can

either exhibit-hop at New Haven's various art galleries or you can tour
the city's historical sites. If you choose the latter, write the New
Haven Preservation Trust, Box 1671, New Haven, Connecticut, and
ask for their "Guide to Historic New Haven." Over fifty historic
buildings are listed in this easy-to-follow walking tour of the city.

Gallery hopping in the city should include the *Munson Gallery*
(closed Sundays and Mondays), the nearby *Creative Arts Workshop
Gallery*, and the *Archetype Photographic Gallery* (on 159 Orange
Street . . . winter hours are Tuesday through Friday from 10–5:00 P.M.
Saturday and Sunday from 1–5:00 P.M., closed Mondays. For summer
hours call 203–776–4454). Each of these galleries exhibit contemporary works by both local and international artists.

Whitlock's Book Barn in Bethany, Connecticut, is open Tuesday
through Sunday from 9–5:00 P.M. If you take Route 69 out of New

Haven, pretty soon you'll be in the sticks. Just before the New Haven/Bethany town line, take a left turn off of Route 69 onto Morris Road. Morris Road will then dead end at Sperry Road, and if you turn right onto Sperry, the book barn is just a few hundred feet off to your right. Whitlock's Book Barn sells used paperbacks and hardcovers. You can browse in the book-cluttered barn or just enjoy the rural setting.

Sperry Falls in Woodbridge, Connecticut (the falls are off of Sperry Road, just about a mile beyond the Bethany/Woodbridge town line) is one of those undisturbed spots local residents are apt to keep quiet about. A quarter-of-a-mile trail descends from a dirt parking lot into the fall's area, and it's here where you can "reflect in tranquility" on nature's bounty. BUT DON'T PICNIC AT THE FALLS. It's just a small isolated area and should be used for either contemplative gazing or romantic trysts.

"Chop Suey" Trips

16. Western Connecticut

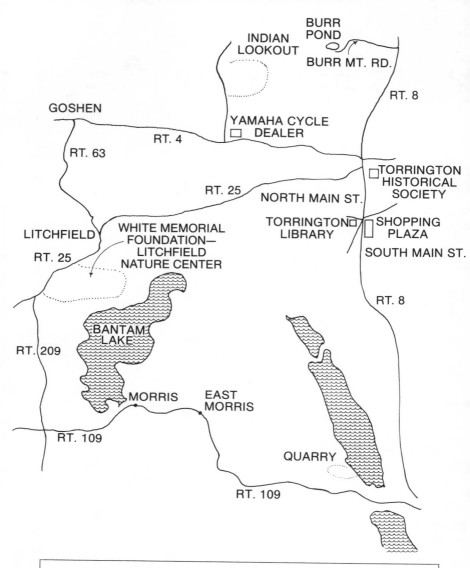

BURR POND

INDIAN LOOKOUT

BURR MT. RD.

RT. 8

GOSHEN

YAMAHA CYCLE DEALER

RT. 4

RT. 63

RT. 25

TORRINGTON HISTORICAL SOCIETY

NORTH MAIN ST.

TORRINGTON LIBRARY

SHOPPING PLAZA

LITCHFIELD

WHITE MEMORIAL FOUNDATION— LITCHFIELD NATURE CENTER

SOUTH MAIN ST.

RT. 25

RT. 8

BANTAM LAKE

RT. 209

MORRIS

EAST MORRIS

RT. 109

QUARRY

RT. 109

HOW TO GET THERE: From New York City take Route 95 into Route 8. Route 8 goes right into the town of Torrington. From Boston, take Route 90 to Route 86. Near Hartford, pick up Route 44 West. From 44 West take Route 25 which will take you into Torrington.

9:30–10:30 A.M.	(Sat. only) Torrington Library Museum, Torrington, Conn.
10:30–11:30 A.M.	The Torrington Historical Society, Torrington, Conn.
11:30–12:30 P.M.	Indian Lookout, Torrington, Conn.
12:30– 1:30 P.M.	Burr Pond State Park, Burrville, Conn.
1:30– 2:30 P.M.	The Litchfield Historical Society, Litchfield, Conn.
2:30– 3:30 P.M.	A Walking Tour of Historic Litchfield, including America's First Law School and the Birthplace of Harriet Beecher Stowe, Litchfield, Conn.

AFTERNOON SITES (Optional)

3:30– 4:30 P.M.	The Litchfield Nature Center and Museum, Litchfield, Conn.
4:30– 6:30 P.M.	The Morris Reservoir Quarry, Morris, Conn.

(This trip can be taken on two separate days or on one long day. If you prefer a leisurely pace, visit the last two afternoon sites separately.)

Eclectic Litchfield

The *Torrington Library Museum* (12 Daycoeton Place, Torrington, Connecticut), this trip's first stop, has an interesting assortment of exhibits. And though the museum is small, its displays of glassware, dolls, Staffordshire plates, and music boxes are all worth seeing. The museum, unfortunately, is only open on Saturdays.

Next, the *Torrington Historical Society Museum* (right on Torrington's Main Street, adjacent to the town's post office) is the former Hotchkiss-Flyer House. Furnishings and rugs of the original manse are here on exhibit. (As you walk into the museum, make sure to note the home's intricately carved oak doors. They're representative of the type of care and artistry that went into the building's construction). For the exact days and hours the museum is open, call 203–482–8260.

To reach *Indian Lookout*, where both rare and native varieties of mountain laurel bloom in the springtime, take Route 4 West (North Elm Street) out of Torrington. Drive only a few miles and then (directly after the Yamaha Motorcycle Dealer), take a right turn. The laurel fields will then be on your right-hand-side at the top of the hill.

From Torrington, head towards Burrville, Connecticut, along Route 8. After arriving in the center of Burrville, turn left at the blinking light. *Burr Pond State Park* will then be just a couple of miles up this road. And surrounded by more than 1,000 acres of state-owned forest, the pond is an excellent midday swimming and picnicking site.

Litchfield, Connecticut, today, a quiet residential community, has one of the least known but most extensive historical pasts of any of New England's small towns. The first law school ever built in the U.S. (Aaron Burr was its first student), as well as the first school to offer higher education to young women, were, in fact, both established in Litchfield.

The town's *Historical Society Museum* (on South Street) is one of the most elaborate town museums in all New England. It serves as a good introduction to Litchfield, and should be the first stop on your historic walking tour of the town. (The museum is open from 2–4:00 P.M., Tuesday through Saturday between March 4 and May 14. From May 15 through October 15, the hours are 11–5:00 P.M. Tuesday through Saturday.)

(If, after touring Litchfield, you're *frip-sated*, it's probably a good time to start returning home. But for those of you who still have some reserves of energy, the following sites are both worth seeing.)

The White Memorial Foundation (just outside of the center of Litchfield, off of Route 25) is one of the best nature centers/museums in the entire country. The preserve includes over 4,000 acres of New England woodland, field, stream, and lake, and the sanctuary's museum offers carefully designed exhibits of regional minerals, butterflies, birds, and mammals. (The museum is open from 9–5:00 P.M., Tuesday through Saturday.)

On Saturdays at 2:00 P.M., there's a free guided nature tour, and in April and May, when all the migrating birds are moving in, free birding tours start on Sunday mornings at 6:30 A.M. and 8:00 A.M.

Mineral collecting is an unadulterated gas. To find worthwhile specimens, you usually have to trek deep into the mountains to some old and abandoned quarry. The exercise, coupled to the sheer fun of gem collecting, makes rockhounding an ideal hobby. (The suspense, too, of "will I or won't I uncover any worthwhile specimens," adds to the enjoyment.)

To give you a feel for the type of isolated spots you'll be visiting as a mineral collector, we've here included one old quarry—the *Morris*

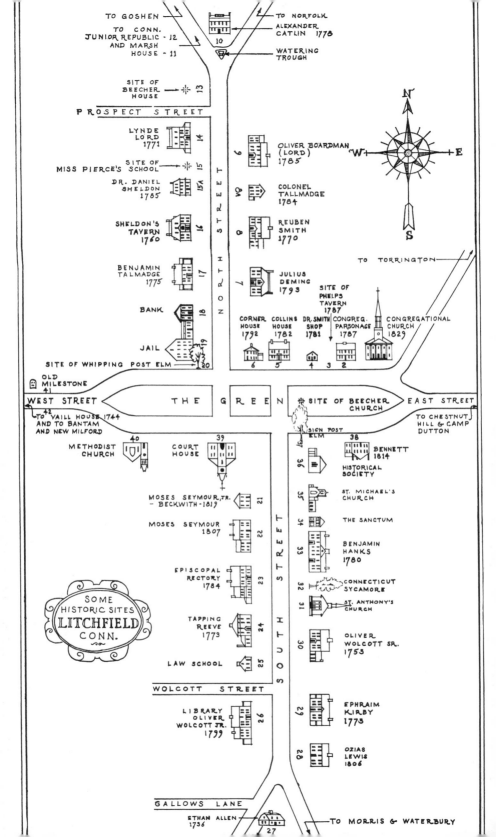

SOME HISTORIC SITES
LITCHFIELD
CONN.

Reservoir Quarry—that's tucked deep in the hills. (Remember: Make sure to bring along a pick-ax and a shovel on this trip for once you reach the site, you'll have to dig around the quarry to unearth any of the smokey quartz crystals this area is noted for.)

If after this expedition (which of course is free) you're a converted rockhound, purchase Ronald Everett Januzzi's "The Mineral Localities of Connecticut and Southeastern New York". Of all the regional guidebooks, this one's by far the best.

DIRECTIONS TO THE MORRIS RESERVOIR QUARRY, MORRIS, CONN.: Take Route 109 through East Morris, Connecticut. When you reach the reservoir (the dam will be on your left and the reservoir control buildings will be on your right) turn left where the brook goes under the road. (The brook is only a couple of hundred feet *before* the reservoir control buildings.) Park your car along the side of the road and on foot, follow the fence posts to the top of the hill. The old quarry will then be west (towards the left) of the dam. (Once on top of the hill, you'll have to cut through some woodlands to locate the quarry.) All in all, despite it sounding like some trans-Siberian trek, it should only take you anywhere from 10–20 minutes to find the quarry.

So good gem hunting and if you find anything valuable, let us know!

More Freebies

Supermarkets inspire free trips. Just walk around any supermarket and for every item that's on the shelves, there's a factory or farm you can visit where the product was made. Places like large commercial bakeries, hot dog manufacturers, maple syrup producers, dairy farms, apple orchards, candy makers, and dozens more all offer free guided tours of their plants.

So first let your fingers do the walking through the yellow pages, and then make a reservation to walk through the factory or farm whose product most intrigues you.

(To give you an idea of just what you'll see on these sort of outings, read our Art Trip, Number 15, New Haven, Connecticut. Here we suggested a visit to Lender's Bagel Bakery in West Haven, Connecticut.)

17. Eastern, Connecticut

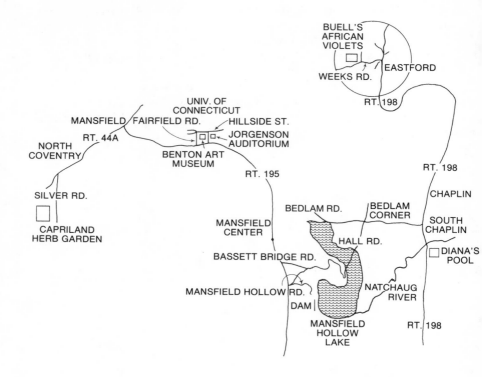

BUELL'S
AFRICAN
VIOLETS

WEEKS RD.

EASTFORD

RT. 198

UNIV. OF
CONNECTICUT

MANSFIELD / FAIRFIELD RD.

HILLSIDE ST.

RT. 44A

JORGENSON
AUDITORIUM

NORTH
COVENTRY

BENTON ART
MUSEUM

RT. 195

RT. 198

CHAPLIN

SILVER RD.

BEDLAM RD.

BEDLAM
CORNER

SOUTH
CHAPLIN

CAPRILAND
HERB GARDEN

MANSFIELD
CENTER

HALL RD.

DIANA'S
POOL

BASSETT BRIDGE RD.

MANSFIELD HOLLOW RD.

NATCHAUG
RIVER

DAM

MANSFIELD
HOLLOW
LAKE

RT. 198

HOW TO GET THERE: From New York City take Route 95 into Route 91 to Hartford. From Hartford pick up Route 44 East. Route 44 goes right near Storrs. From Boston take Route 90 and pick up Route 86 around Sturbridge. When Route 86 intersects with Route 195, take Route 195 right into Storrs.

10:00–12:00 P.M.	The William Benton Museum of Art, The Jorgensen Auditorium Gallery, A Brief Walking Tour of The University of Connecticut, Storrs, Conn.
12:00– 1:00 P.M.	Capriland Herb Farm, North Coventry, Conn.
1:00– 2:30 P.M.	Mansfield Hollow Dam and Recreation Area, Mansfield, Conn.
2:30– 3:30 P.M.	Diana's Pool, Chaplin, Conn.
3:30– 4:30 P.M.	Buell's African Violets, Eastford Center, Conn.
4:30– 6:00 P.M.	Natchaug State Forest, Eastford, Conn.

An Idyllic Romp in "Colonial" America

As far as colleges being superannuated institutions, they are. Just ask any unemployed college grad. But despite our nation's colleges and universities being only occasionally useful to their students, they're almost always invaluable stopovers for day frippers. With all their museums, free cultural events (including concerts, plays, and lectures), our institutions of higher learning are nothing less than freebie havens.

The William Benton Museum of Art on the campus of the University of Connecticut in Storrs, Connecticut (open June 1 through August 11 from 10–4:00 P.M. on Monday through Saturday; Sunday 1–5:00 P.M.; and during the school year—Monday through Saturday from 10–4:30 P.M. and Sunday 1–5:00 P.M.) is an excellent art gallery whose exhibitions are continually changing. And nearby, *The Jorgenson Auditorium Art Gallery* also offers off-beat contemporary displays.

(Whenever you visit a college campus, make sure to see a list of the day's activities. Usually, there'll be some lecture or concert that will be worth attending.)

Capriland Herb Farm on Silver Street in North Coventry, Connecticut (open Monday through Saturday 9–5:00 P.M.; Sunday 12–5:00 P.M.) consists of fourteen carefully designed herb gardens. (One of the gardens even displays every herb mentioned in Shakespeare's works.) You can spend a restful and scent-ful hour here, leisurely wandering around the well-cared for gardens.

A good site for this trip's picnic lunch is *The Mansfield Hollow Dam and Recreation Area* in Mansfield, Connecticut. The dam, built in 1944 by the U.S. Army Corps of Engineers, is a massive wall of

107

concrete, 12,420 feet long and 68 feet high. And near the dam, on the banks of the Natchaug River, free parking and picnicking facilities are available.

Diana's Pool, where the Natchaug River rumbles over a series of huge boulders, is in Chaplin, Connecticut. (To reach this site proceed from the Chaplin Post Office on Route 198 for about one-and-one-half miles. Then, directly before you reach a small concrete bridge, on your left-hand-side will be a dirt parking area. Park here and follow the trails to the rapids.) This entire area, with its water falls and granite boulders, is perfect for meditating/hiking/mountain climbing/romantic trysts/chemically or naturally induced highs/and as a cure for any and every emotional affliction.

Buell's African Violets (located one-sixth of a mile from Eastford Center, Connecticut off of Weeks Road) is a commercial greenhouse that grows over 500 varieties of violets. Over 140,000 plants burst into bloom here in August and December. So it's best to plan your visit to the greenhouses for either of these two months.

And your last stop on this romp through eastern Connecticut is the *Natchaug State Forest* in Eastford, Connecticut. Here fishing, hiking, and picnicking facilities are all available. Also, during the springtime, you'll probably be able to spot some wild violets growing on the forest's floor. The wild variety are of course, quite different from those you'll see in Buell's greenhouses.

18. Southeastern Connecticut

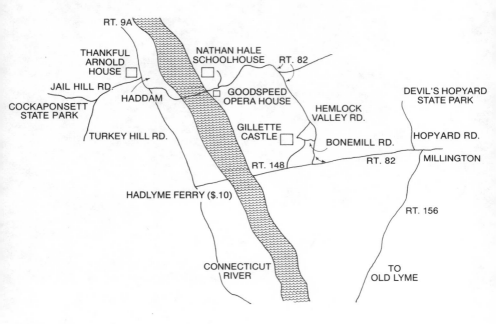

HOW TO GET THERE: From New York City take Route 95 to Old Lyme, Connecticut. At Old Lyme, pick up Route 156 heading towards Millington, Connecticut. From Boston, take Route 95, and near Old Lyme, Connecticut, pick up Route 156 heading towards Millington.

9:00–10:30 A.M.	Devil's Hopyard State Park, Millington, Conn.
10:30–12:30 P.M.	Gillette Castle, South of East Haddam, Conn.
12:30– 1:30 P.M.	Goodspeed Opera House, Nathan Hale's "Little Red School House," Old Victorian Homes, East Haddam, Conn.
1:30– 2:00 P.M.	(Optional jaunt) Old Church Pottery, Haddam, Conn.
2:00– 3:30 P.M.	(Optional jaunt) Cockaponset State Forest and Russell Pond, West Haddam, Conn.
3:30– 4:30 P.M.	Thankful Arnold House, Haddam, Conn.
4:30– 5:30 P.M.	Haddam Meadows and the Yankee Atomic Power Plant, Haddam, Conn.

An Historical, Art, and Nature Trip

Devil's Hopyard State Park, off of Route 82 near Millington, Connecticut, has a satori-inducing waterfall. "Satori," in Zen Buddhist scriptures, is a term describing that pure state of being where only the fullness of the present moment is experienced.

By watching the ever changing/ever constant waterfall at Devil's Hopyard (and I mean really watching it—for anywhere from a half-an-hour to two hours)—you just might get a taste for the Zen satori experience.

Heading west from the park along Route 82 (towards East Haddam), you'll soon see signs for the *Gillette Castle and State Park*. Follow these signs to the park's entrance.

Gillette Castle, built in 1914 by William Gillette—a turn-of-the-century actor—is a massive and eccentric stone structure. Consisting of granite walls—all of them four to five feet in thickness—it was here (overlooking the Connecticut River), that the actor Gillette let his architectural fantasies loose. And though it costs $.50 to tour the castle's interior, admission to both the park and the castle sites are free. So you can walk along the castle's porch and take in the transcendent vistas *free*-of-charge.

From the castle area, follow the walking trails towards the *Hadlyme Ferry* slip. Here, for $.10, you can take a round-trip ferry ride across the Connecticut River. (The ferry runs continuously from April 1 through November 30.)

East Haddam, Connecticut had its hey-day in the "gay nineties." As a cultural center, featuring the internationally acclaimed *Good-*

speed Opera House, the town used to host droves of well-to-do New Yorkers and Bostonians. Today, you can view the 1847 opera house which has become a theater that specializes in the production of native American musicals.

The entire town of East Haddam is filled with other gems of Victorian architecture. Along the town's main street (Route 82), be sure to stop and look at some of these extravagantly constructed buildings.

A *"Little Red School House"* where Nathan Hale taught (Hale, if you can remember your easily forgotten history lessons, was the American patriot who regretted he had "but one life to lose for his country") is also located in the town of East Haddam. To reach the school-house, just turn left off of Route 82 onto Route 149, and then turn onto the winding blacktop road that's directly before East Haddam's church.

Next, to reach *Cockaponset State Park* take Jail Hill Road out of the town of Haddam and turn onto Turkey Hill Road. Off of Turkey Hill Road then turn onto Filley Road. The park's entrance will then be just a short drive from this intersection.

The park, besides having a number of picnic areas and nature trails, also has a swimming spot—*Russell Pond.*

In the town of Haddam, open Saturdays and Sundays (June through September) from 2:30–5:00 P.M. is the *Thankful Arnold House.* The house, built in the late 1700's, exhibits Windsor chairs, Queen Anne furnishings, and Staffordshire dishes. In addition, an herb and kitchen garden exactly duplicating those of the late eighteenth-century, are on the premises.

The last stop on this "Chop Suey Trip" through southeastern Connecticut is *last* both in a chronological sense and possibly even in a prophetic sense as well; *prophetic,* unfortunately, in the Doomsday sense of the word.

Haddam Meadows, in Haddam, Connecticut, is an isolated spot overlooking the Connecticut River. It also, though, overlooks the *Yankee Atomic Power Plant.* This imposing structure, camouflaged on the banks of the Connecticut River, was one of the first nuclear power plants ever built in the northeastern United States. And being that nuclear energy, according to many prestigious scientists, hasn't yet been technologically perfected, the concrete power plant sits, for my tastes, a bit too precariously on the banks of the river.

But Haddam Meadows, despite the imposing vision of the power plant, is a good spot to rest before starting on your trip back home.

OPTIONAL JAUNTS: If you have time, the two optional sites listed on this trip's suggested itinerary are both worthwhile. *The Old Church Pottery*, which is the showroom and studio of a Haddam,

Connecticut potter, gives you a first-hand glimpse into the ancient craft of pottery. And *Cockaponset State Forest*, in West Haddam, (assuming you haven't already overdosed on this trip's natural settings), is a good place to spend some restful hours. See map for directions to both these sites.

19. Worcester, Massachusetts

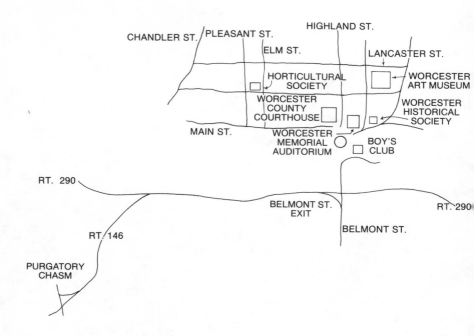

HOW TO GET THERE: From New York City take Route 95 into Route 91. Out of Hartford, Conn. pick up Route 86. Route 86 runs into Route 90 and Route 90 will take you near Worcester. From Boston take Route 90 West into Worcester.

9:00–11:00 A.M.	Purgatory Chasm State Reservation, South of Worcester, near Sutton, Mass.
11:30– 2:00 P.M.	Worcester Art Museum, Worcester, Mass.
2:00– 3:00 P.M.	Worcester Historical Society Museum, Worcester, Mass.
3:00– 4:00 P.M.	Worcester County Horticultural Society, Worcester, Mass.

An Old City and Purgatory Chasm

Purgatory Chasm (located twelve miles south of Worcester, Massachusetts, just off of Route 146) is one of the most eerie landscapes imaginable. Geologically, the area is a deep split in the earth, filled with hundreds of granite boulders. And literally, as you walk through the dark chasm, a science fiction/extraterrestrial feeling permeates your being. It's as if you're in the bowels of the universe; part of some long journey towards "the center of the earth."

(Since the path leading through the area involves maneuvering across some fairly precarious rock formations, the chasm isn't really the safest place for a family outing. Safety aside, though, Purgatory Chasm is one of New England's more bizarre terrains and if you're at all intrepid, make it a point to frip here.)

To reach the *Worcester Art Museum* (55 Salisbury Street) from Purgatory Chasm, take Route 146 North towards Worcester. Then pick up Route 290 East and finally, off of Route 290 East, use exit 17 (Belmont Street).

The museum (open Tuesday through Saturdays, 10–5:00 P.M.; Sundays 2–6:00 P.M.) consists of four floors—and each of them is filled with both ancient and contemporary art treasures. Egyptian, Chinese, and Indian paintings and sculptures, along with twentieth century Cubist and surrealist works abound. On the first floor is also a Benedictine monastery's priory that was reassembled after it had been razed in France. The priory, with its marble arches and stained-glass windows, is filled with a subtle and peaceful presence.

Nearby, the *Worcester Historical Society* (open Monday through Friday, from 10–3:00 P.M.) offers a museum featuring colonial American artifacts. Ship models, elaborate Victorian doll houses, old muskets, Civil War uniforms, and a collection of early American farm tools are all on exhibit.

The *Worcester County Horticultural Society* (at 30 Elm Street; open 10–12:00 P.M., 1–4:00 P.M., Monday through Friday) offers free and open-to-the-public flower shows throughout the year. Roses, irises, lilies and dahlias are each featured at the exhibitions. You can call 617–752–4274 for specific information about any one of the shows or write: The Worcester County Horticultural Society, 30 Elm Street, Worcester, Massachusetts. (Enclose a self-addressed stamped envelope to receive an exhibition schedule.)

When there's no show at the society, you can visit the main headquarters and there spend time with the over 5,000 volumes of horticulture-related works that comprise the society's library.

On Making Each Trip Count

Homework is usually a drag. But if you don't do it, you're just not going to be prepared for the day's lessons. Same thing with fripping. If you don't take a few moments out to do some preparatory work, then you'll certainly miss at least part of what a certain frip might offer.

So if you're going out on an historical trip, go to the library beforehand and read up on a specific area's history. Or for a nature trip, familiarize yourself with that region's flora and fauna. Simply, the more homework you do, the better informed will be your journey. (But don't suffocate your fellow frippers with your newly-acquired knowledge. That sort of thing can quickly make a frip an egregious drag.)

Also, study maps; for maps are invaluable tools—always filled with extraordinarily eccentric scraps of knowledge.

And before leaving on your frip—just when you're about to turn the car key—take a few luxurious deep breaths. Then look at your co-frippers. If everything then seems fine, begin fripping.

... And always remember: It's more important that you enjoy yourself than to compulsively visit every site that's on the itinerary.

20. Western Massachusetts

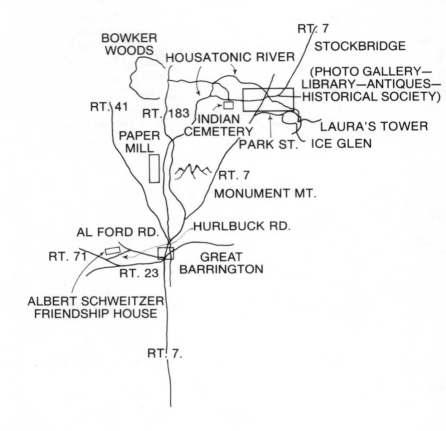

HOW TO GET THERE: From New York City take the Taconic State Parkway North to the Berkshire/New York State Thruway exit. This road will take you right into the Stockbridge area. From Boston simply stay on Route 90 across the entire length of the state.

9:30–10:30 A.M.	The Stockbridge Library Museum, Stockbridge, Mass.
10:30–11:30 A.M.	Image Gallery, Antique Shops, Stockbridge, Mass.
11:30– 1:30 P.M.	Ice Glen and Laurel Tower, Stockbridge, Mass.
1:30– 2:30 P.M.	Bowker's Woods, Glendale, Mass.
2:30– 3:30 P.M.	(Optional) A Tour of a Paper Mill, near Great Barrington, Mass.
3:00– 5:00 P.M.	The Albert Schweitzer Friendship House, Great Barrington, Mass. (Call 413–528–3124 for an appointment before going.)

Art, Nature, Industry and the Human Spirit

"I well remember as I passed through Stockbridge, how much
I was struck by the beauty of the smooth green meadows on
the banks of that lovely river, the Housatonic, whose gently
flowing waters seemed tinged with gold and crimson of the
trees that overhung them."

—William Cullen Bryant

Stockbridge, Massachusetts, a classically quaint New England village in the Berkshire Hills, has for years been a thriving center for cultural events. The Berkshire Music Festival, one of this country's top musical events, takes place at Tanglewood—a 210 acre estate located just north of Stockbridge. The painter, Norman Rockwell, whose realistically depicted mom-and-apple-pie pictures are world famous, also works from a studio situated right in the heart of the town. And countless other authors, playwrights, and craftsmen all make their home in this lush area.

A good place to start fripping in Stockbridge is the *Stockbridge Town Library*. Here, in the library's basement, is an excellent small museum, consisting solely of historical artifacts of Stockbridge.

From the museum, walk up Main Street until you reach the *Image Gallery*. (Open Monday through Saturday from 10–5:00 P.M.; Sundays 11–4:00 P.M.) Primarily contemporary artists and photographers exhibit their works here, and even if you don't intend on making any art purchases, stop in and look around. Similarly, there are a number of *antique shops* in Stockbridge—and all of them are worth seeing.

123

Leaving the town on Route 7 South and turning left on Park Street, proceed a-half-mile until you reach *Ice Glen* and *Laurel Tower*. Here, where the Housatonic River runs through the mountains, a group of interconnecting walking trails create a lush hike through the New England woods.

Bowker's Woods in Glendale, Massachusetts (since its location is utterly obscure you'll have to ask at the Glendale Post Office for the exact directions) is an isolated, practically remote site. If you're adventuresome and enjoy having acres and acres of woods to yourself, then picnic here. Its remoteness all but insures absolute privacy.

(A possible side-trip on this already mad melange of freebies is a tour of a paper mill. There are a number of such mills along the shores of the Housatonic River and most of them welcome visitors. *The Rising Paper Company*, only a few miles outside of Stockbridge and Great Barrington, offers free guided tours as long as prior arrangements are made. To arrange a tour, call 413–274–3345 and ask to speak with Robert Montana, the mill's office manager.)

The Albert Schweitzer Friendship House and Library (on Hurlburt Road in Great Barrington, Massachusetts) is a very special site. It was back in 1967 that Mrs. Erica Anderson, a friend and disciple of Schweitzer's, first founded the Friendship House. Its purpose was to "promote among all people, especially the young, the understanding and the practice of Dr. Schweitzer's philosophy 'Reverence for Life'." And today, just by feeling the calm, "loveful" atmosphere that suffuses this forty acre area, you'll immediately know that at least part of the Friendship House's original aim has been realized. A documentary movie of Schweitzer's life is shown at the Friendship House, and as both an enjoyable cinema experience, as well as a divinely-inspired and inspiring work, it's more than worth your time.

On the grounds of the Friendship House, too, are a number of walking trails. And along any one of these trails, you'll periodically be seeing brief quotes of Schweitzer's that have been painted on wooden signposts.

One sign, in particular, intrigued me. And because it obliquely expresses a lot of why this guidebook was ever written, I'd like to now end our book with the quote.

"Everyone must work to live but the purpose of life is to serve and to show compassion and the will to help others. Only then have we become true human beings."

... So enjoy fripping. ...

And thank you for allowing us to serve you.